Against Progress

Žižek's Essays

Series Editor: Liza Thompson

Žižek's Essays showcase the best of Slavoj Žižek's thought and writing in short, punchy collections of essays. Carefully curated to chart the intellectual journeys of one of the world's prominent philosophers, each book brings together writings addressing the most urgent issues facing the contemporary subject. Written with Žižek's characteristic verve, expansiveness, erudition and imagination, the essays combine the enduring Žižekian preoccupations of Marxism, psychoanalysis, contemporary politics and film with emerging themes—particle physics, new theories of history, authenticity in the age of AI, war and ecological collapse in all its catastrophic forms. *Žižek's Essays* invite both seasoned readers and new discoverers to experience thinking life, politics and history through the idiosyncratic and topsy-turvy brilliance of the ultimate philosopher for a world turned upside down.

Also Available from Bloomsbury

Christian Atheism, Slavoj Žižek
Freedom, Slavoj Žižek
Surplus-Enjoyment, Slavoj Žižek
Hegel in a Wired Brain, Slavoj Žižek
Sex and the Failed Absolute, Slavoj Žižek
Disparities, Slavoj Žižek
Antigone, Slavoj Žižek

Against Progress

Slavoj Žižek

BLOOMSBURY ACADEMIC
LONDON • NEW YORK • OXFORD • NEW DELHI • SYDNEY

BLOOMSBURY ACADEMIC
Bloomsbury Publishing Plc, 50 Bedford Square, London, WC1B 3DP, UK
Bloomsbury Publishing Inc, 1359 Broadway, 12th Floor, New York, NY 10018, USA
Bloomsbury Publishing Ireland, 29 Earlsfort Terrace, Dublin 2, D02 AY28, Ireland

First published in Great Britain 2025
Reprinted in 2025 (eight times)

Design: Ben Anslow
Photo © jeromefavrestudio

A catalogue record for this book is available from the British Library.
A catalog record for this book is available from the Library of Congress.

ISBN: PB: 978-1-3505-1585-7
ePDF: 978-1-3505-1586-4
eBook: 978-1-3505-1587-1

Series: Žižek's Essays

Typeset by RefineCatch Limited, Bungay, Suffolk
Printed and bound in Great Britain

For product safety related questions contact
productsafety@bloomsbury.com.

To find out more about our authors and books visit
www.bloomsbury.com and sign up for our newsletters.

Contents

Editors' Note

Living in a world in which new possibilities for annihilation seem to be proliferating – global conflict, the confirmed climate crisis leading to ecological collapse, the rise of the far right, and the crumbling of many of the pillars of the liberal social democratic order we took for granted – 'progress' seems, in some ways, a quaint concept to seize upon. A word redolent of Victorian reformers, earnest Fabians, and 1950s 'imagineers' envisioning a bright and shining future, it seems at first glance an odd preoccupation for times in which all we can know for certain is that tomorrow *will not* be like today.

But as Slavoj Žižek persistently argues in this unsettling book, we do not *behave* as if we know that the days of our old certainties are numbered. We go to work, pursue our individual goals, drive cars, eat meat, throw away what we no longer want, have children, just as if the planet is not burning, as if its resources are not exhausted, as if our societies are not sliding into neo-fascist oligarchies. Wedged inexorably in what Žižek, drawing on Jacques Lacan, calls the 'fetishistic split', we have lost the ability to imagine a future other than the one that we know for certain will not materialize, the one in which our way of life continues without destabilization. These essays chart the absences left by the loss of old certainties, even such basic certainties as the survival of the human species; and the ways in which the void left by lost futures is filled by demagogues of all types, making disingenuous appeals to 'traditional' values to bolster their claim to define what the future can be.

Characteristically, Žižek finds that the only way to address the idea of progress is to thoroughly and ruthlessly deconstruct it, pursuing it through its various protean forms. 'Progress and

Vicissitudes' sets the tone by exposing, mercilessly and not without some fiendish delight, the 'squashed dead birds' which are the inevitable, unpleasant offsets of attempts to forcibly create a better world for other people. It is not merely corporate machinations or the nightmarish visions of neoliberalism which are exposed as hiding squalid, violent realities, either. In 'Against Progress', one of the most helpful, leftist visions of what progress might look like – the eco-Marxism of Kohei Saito – is shown to be fatally flawed in its reliance on humans being something other than they are. Not for the last time, Žižek calls for a rehabilitation of planning, showing that slowing down and decentralizing, appealing as they might sound, are not the answer to a rat-king of global crises gathering pace and power. Nor is racing to catch-up with them in a desperate rush towards annihilation ('Acceleration').

None of this is merely intellectual; there is a visceral panic haunting this book. It is vividly conjured in 'Worsting', where our dread of regression exposes itself in the resurrection of the 'obscene paternal figure' of the Strongman, patriarchal authority's compulsion to persist combined with our desperate attachment to old certainties. Yet Žižek sympathizes with this desperation, this dread: such sympathy, such radical solidarity with the least wanted aspects of our collective selves – the bin juice, dead rats, deadly bacteria and severed limbs, the horrific, collateral of the way we are living – is the matter of 'We Are Biomass'. A different kind of reckoning takes place in 'Holographic History', where a seemingly abstract thought-experiment – is our world a hologram? – becomes a melancholic confrontation with images of what might have been, and with the unsettling role that chance plays in the collapse of potentials into leaden reality. And yet, as in all these essays, there is a strange kind of revitalizing possibility that comes from interrogating ideas of inevitability; if it could have been different, it can – perhaps – always already be different too.

Whatever form it takes, progress is encountered as an idea in crisis. It is a concept at war with its own foundations in the reason of the Enlightenment and the imperialism that underpinned even Karl Marx's formulations of human historical teleology, embattled by Western neo-liberal notions of the 'end of history'. Progress *has* to be encountered as fragmented, partial and perpetually undermining the universalist pretensions that once formed its very core. It is this sense of constant rupturing that makes the form of this book – that of the essay – so vital. These are places to explore and expand, to attack and retreat (in Žižek-approved Leninist fashion), to encounter both desolation and a fractured kind of hope. These pieces speak to a tension, an irreconcilability of feelings where, in the end, we both believe and do not believe things can get better. As Žižek writes in 'Civil War', expanding on Franz Kafka's maxim: 'There is hope . . . just not for us.' Or at least, not as we are now.

Amidst the warnings against hypocrisy and fake self-criticism in 'Authority' we are perhaps given the most concrete glimpse of something that, for Žižek, constitutes authentic progress. In giving short shrift to claims to 'authority' which derive from an objective, eternal truth, he finds in Soren Kierkegaard an unlikely ally. In the Kierkegaardian vision of transformation as neither gradual teleological process nor isolated redemptive moment but as 'repetitive movement', we glimpse the lineaments of a revolution which embraces failure, incompleteness: which is always starting again. We have no place to land, no ground upon which to stand still and no end in sight but we do have curiosity, an insatiable thirst for mischief and delight, a capacity to critique both ourselves and the structures which threaten to swamp us. In Žižek's eclectic, enlivening prose is found an affirmative response to Socrates' call to endlessly repeat a question, a model for our own capacity for that affirmative response. For him, progress is a state of vigilance, a continual resistance to complacency, a paradoxical dive further into what we are driven most desperately to escape – what we ourselves are – which creates the possibility of transformation. It is in working with the bizarre mechanisms of denial and doublethink with which we navigate our reality and embracing the inevitability of utter destruction that hope (if there is any) lies; this is the oddly optimistic note on which 'Disavowal' ends the book.

Because *Against Progress* is, ultimately, an optimistic book; optimistic in its energy, its anger, its resistance to passive drift and entropy. It is exhilarating to be along for the ride as Žižek pounces on a concept or formulation, sucks the juices out of it, and moves on to the next, from quantum mechanics and the mysterious entanglements of subatomic particles to the emancipatory potential of South Korean 'web sosoeol' and the inadvertent political commentary of Hollywood blockbusters, via Einstein, Freud, Adorno, Lacan, the Buddha and, of course, Hegel. And there are jokes, of course. Dirty ones. Being challenged, being surprised, being maddened is part of what's best about reading Žižek; and each one of these pieces can feel like a gauntlet flung down. Žižek shows us that the second we rest on the laurels of any insufficiently examined assumption, the instant we are comfortable, we lose our potential to act as revolutionary subjects. Revolution is not a transcendent, shining moment, nor a linear process (or even a progress), but a constant beginning again. That is what these pieces do; begin again and again, from a different angle, applying a different kind of conceptual leverage, worrying away at the intractable, sometimes reeling away blood-spattered, but always, always, returning to the fray. And not only because the alternative is all too thinkable.

Liza Thompson and Hannah Wilks

Progress and its Vicissitudes

Early in Christopher Nolan's *The Prestige*, a magician performs a trick with a small bird which disappears in a cage flattened on the table. A small boy in the audience starts to cry, distraught that the bird was killed. The magician approaches him and finishes the trick, gently producing a living bird out of his hand – but the boy is not convinced, insisting that this must be another bird, the dead bird's brother. After the show, we see the magician alone, putting a bird squashed into the trash where many other dead birds lie. The boy was right. The trick could not be performed without violence and death, but it relies for its effectiveness upon concealing the squalid, broken residue of what has been sacrificed, disposing of it where no one who matters will see. Therein resides the basic premise of a dialectical notion of progress: when a new higher stage arrives, *there must be a squashed bird somewhere.*

The Squashed Birds of Progress

The first thing to renounce is thus any notion of the global linear progress of humanity, whether formulated by Karl Marx, postulated by liberals like Francis Fukuyama (who declared the end of history) or dominated by Enlightenment dialectics. Marx's overall vision of history is that of a linear succession of 'progressive' modes of social development from primitive societies through the Asiatic mode of production, slavery, feudalism, capitalism to socialism and communism. Problems arise almost immediately with the historical dynamic Marx envisioned; to start with, the notion of an 'Asiatic mode of production' is clearly problematic (it is an empty category into which Marx threw whatever didn't fit his Eurocentric logic of history, and thus in itself a receptacle for squashed dead birds). As for socialism, Rosa Luxemburg's claim 'the future will be socialism or barbarism' proved to be wrong also: what we got in Stalinism was a socialist barbarian, and the corpses are still being counted. As for liberalism, its state of crisis is obvious, so much so that even Fukuyama has renounced his notion of the end of history.

There should be no holds barred in the pursuit of squashed birds. Russia and China like to present themselves as partisans of a new multi-centric world order in which all ways of life will coexist as equal and in which Western colonial economic and ideological domination will finally be swept away. In this rhetoric we might see whole cages of squashed birds swept aside with the West, not only economic and political but also the flattening of feminism, gay rights and general human freedoms. A fairly recent example might be the debate that took place in the Ugandan parliament in February 2023 as the legislature contemplated a further toughening of the anti-gay law – where the most radical proponents demanded the death penalty, or at least life imprisonment, for those caught in the act. Anita Among, speaker of the parliament, stated: 'You are either with us, or you're with the Western world.'[1] We live in an era of *unholy alliances*, collaborations and conjunctions of ideological forces which disrupt the standard binary of Left and Right. Feminist, gay and trans struggles are denounced as an instrument of Western ideological colonialism used to undermine African identity. If this type of thinking continues to be allowed to define the debate, the possibility of being a gay Ugandan, a feminist Ugandan, a trans Ugandan can be redefined out of existence; another casualty of a narrow definition of 'progress'.

The miserable reality is that the promise of decolonization can be co-opted as a screen for other processes, its liberatory potential caught in the vicelike grip of a too-rigid definition of what moving forward means, and suffocated. The people of numerous African countries, from Angola to Zimbabwe, exist under more or less corrupt social systems in which the gap between the 'masters' and the poor majority – the gap in wealth, in power, in privileges and freedom – is arguably even wider than under colonial rule. 'Decolonization' in these circumstances can function almost as a metaphor for the emergence of new class-based hierarchies. While there are, of course, a myriad of arguments that one can advance against any suggestion that things were 'better' under colonial rule, if we fail to recognize the potential for decolonial movements to be absorbed into problematic regimes, the new Right will do it for us (as they are already doing in the case of South Africa, bloviating about the inability of Black people to run the country 'properly'.) Mao said: 'Revolution is not a dinner party.' But what if the reality after the revolution is even *less* of a dinner party? This in no way implies that we should abandon progress – we should rather redefine it, and the first step towards doing so is to be able to acknowledge uncomfortable realities, even those which appear squalid and mangled, and especially those we find shameful and grievous and which seem to have no remedy. We need less squashed birds hidden in trunks while we applaud the false living bird distracting us from capitalist corruption and authoritarian power.

The two articles Marx wrote on India in 1893 ('The British Rule in India' and 'The Future Results of British Rule in India'), usually dismissed by postcolonial scholars as embarrassing cases of Marx's 'Eurocentrism', are today more interesting than ever. Marx outlines, without restraint, the brutality and exploitative hypocrisy of the British colonization of India, right up to the systematic use of torture prohibited in the West but 'outsourced' to Indians (really there is nothing new under the sun – these were the Guantanamos of nineteenth-century British India): 'The profound hypocrisy and inherent barbarism of bourgeois civilization lies unveiled before our eyes, turning from its home, where it assumes respectable forms, to the colonies, where it goes naked.'[2] All Marx adds is that

> England has broken down the entire framework of Indian society, without any symptoms of reconstitution yet appearing. This loss of his old world, with no gain of a new one, imparts a particular kind of melancholy to the present misery of the Hindoo, and separates Hindostan, ruled by Britain, from all its ancient traditions, and from the whole of its past history. [...] England, it is true, in causing a social revolution in Hindostan, was actuated only by the vilest interests, and was stupid in her manner of enforcing them. But that is not the question. The question is, can mankind fulfil its destiny without a fundamental

> revolution in the social state of Asia? If not, whatever may have been the crimes of England she was the unconscious tool of history in bringing about that revolution.[3]

Despite the mention of 'destiny', one should not wholly dismiss the notion of the 'unconscious tool of history' as naive teleology, an ends-justify-the-means fatalistic 'trust into the Cunning of Reason which makes even the vilest crimes instruments of progress'. The point Marx is making is simply that the British colonization of India created conditions for the double liberation of India: from the constraints of its own tradition as well as from colonization itself . . . Today, of course, such a standpoint appears all too naive – now we know how the British colonizers destroyed local industries in India and provoked havoc with tens of millions dead. Of course, we would never say that the horrors of colonization were worth the price of progressing towards some nebulous utopian future. A much more modest stance should be adopted: Great Britain's actions in India were inexcusable and the direct outcome a devastating catastrophe; however, once this catastrophe happened, it opened up a new path for India. That 'however' is an uncomfortable adverb to dwell in, but it remains open to hope as neater historical narratives do not.

When Theodor Adorno and Max Horkheimer delineate the contours of the emerging late-capitalist 'administered world' (*verwaltete Welt*), they are presenting it as coinciding with barbarism, as the point at which civilization itself returns to barbarism. A kind of negative telos of the whole progress of Enlightenment, as the Nietzschean kingdom of the Last Men: 'One has one's little pleasure for the day and one's little pleasure for the night: but one has a regard for health. "We have invented happiness," say the last men, and they blink.'[4] At the same time, Adorno and Horkheimer nevertheless warn against the more direct 'ontic' catastrophes (different forms of terror, etc.). The liberal-democratic society of Last Men is thus unimaginably awful, the only problem being that all other societies are worse, so that the choice appears as one between bad and worse (or a rock and a hard place). The ambiguity is here irreducible: on the one hand, the 'administered world' is the final catastrophic outcome of the Enlightenment; on the other hand, the 'normal' societal path is continually threatened by catastrophes, from war and terror to ecological disasters. We are required to battle these 'ontic' catastrophes (what we experience as catastrophic events in our social reality) while simultaneously bearing in mind that the ultimate catastrophe is the apparently 'normal' structures and rhythms of the 'administered world'. In other words, we are walking a kind of Moebius path: if we progress far enough on one side, we reach our starting point again. Does the same not hold for progressivism in general? After centuries in which visionaries of all stripes dreamed of what humanity might achieve together. the only indubitable 'progressive' goal that humanity can pursue today, in view of ecological and other threats, is to simply *survive*.

The possibilities and pitfalls of technological and scientific advancement have been the stuff of centuries' worth of dreaming about human progress, yet here too we find ourselves treading a viciously circular path. Free development, experimentation and research leads to Artificial Intelligence, which not only threatens to supplant the human mind but is *intended* specifically to overcome its limitations, to replicate humanity without its frailties. Leaving aside more abstract questions about what this would look like and mean should it be achieved, one does not have to look very far for the dead birds littering the path to 'progress' like autumn leaves, from the astronomical energy costs burdening a burning planet to the people whose jobs will increasingly be done by AI. This is what blind commitment to an uncritically adopted idea of 'progress' looks like; proponents of AI talk about the freedom it brings, but are vague on freedom from what, for who and what for. Freedom for humanity to dedicate itself to leisure, art or meditation? Or freedom for an oligarchy of technocrats from the slightest tethering to the social contract, in exchange for reducing humanity to a cog in the endless self-reproduction of AI?

This brings us to the relationship between progress and freedom. The axiom of modern philosophy is that progress is, at its most fundamental, progress in freedom. (This is how Hegel conceives the development of the entire history of humanity: in Oriental despotism only the despot is free; in antique slavery only the few are free; and with Christianity all are free.) However, problems with the definition of freedom explode here from the very beginning.

Within the Enlightenment tradition, there is true freedom only if all are equally free, while for conservative liberals equality limits freedom; then there is the opposition between individual freedom and collective freedom (freedom of a nation advocated by fascism). For socialists, freedom is actual only when its material and institutional conditions are present (free education and press, healthcare), while for liberal conservatives, such measures already limit the full freedom of individuals (recall how US Republicans opposed Obamacare, claiming that it will limit the freedom to choose your own doctor).

The issue is further complicated by the post-1960s shift away from economic and political freedom to cultural freedom. Why, after the 1960s, have so many problems come to be perceived as problems of intolerance, not as problems of inequality, exploitation, injustice? Why is the proposed remedy tolerance, not emancipation, political struggle, even armed struggle? The immediate answer is the 'culturalization of politics', in which political differences, differences conditioned by political inequality, economic exploitation and so forth are neutralized into 'cultural' differences, different 'ways of life', which are something given, something that cannot be overcome, but merely 'tolerated'. The response to this shift comes in Benjaminian terms: *from culturalization of politics to politicization of culture*. The cause of this culturalization is the retreat or failure of direct political solutions, such as the welfare state, socialist projects, attempts to *do*, to build. Tolerance is the post-political ersatz of these solutions:

> The retreat from more substantive visions of justice heralded by the promulgation of tolerance today is part of a more general depoliticization of citizenship and power and retreat from political life itself. The cultivation of tolerance as a political end implicitly constitutes a rejection of politics as a domain in which conflict can be productively articulated and addressed, a domain in which citizens can be transformed by their participation.[5]

The squashed dead bird here is politics itself. And this bird remains squashed even after the rise of the Rightist new populism: the conflict between the liberal centre and the new Right, political as it may appear, still excludes emancipatory politics proper.

Progress as Redemption

How, then, should we orient ourselves in this mess? Our starting point should be that there is no such thing as progress in general: progress is the inner development of a system, the gradual actualization of its potentials, so it all depends on which system serves as a point of reference. The most radical vision of (quite literally) universal progress was proposed by the so-called 'bio-cosmism', a strange combination of vulgar materialism and Gnostic spirituality which formed the obscene secret teaching of Soviet Marxism. Repressed out of public sight in the central (Stalinist) period of the Soviet state, bio-cosmism was openly propagated only in the first and in the last two decades of the Soviet rule; its main theses are that the goals of religion (collective paradise, overcoming of all suffering, full individual immortality, resurrection of the dead, victory over time and death, conquest of space far beyond the solar system) can be realized in terrestrial life through the development of modern science and technology. In the future, not only will sexual difference be abolished, with the rise of chaste post-humans perpetuating themselves through direct bio-technical reproduction; it will also be possible to resurrect all the dead of the past (establishing their biological formula through their remains and then re-engendering them), thus even erasing all past injustices, 'undoing' past suffering and destruction. In this bright bio-political communist future, not only humans, but also animals, all living beings, will participate in a directly collectivized Reason of the cosmos. (Note that today's proponents of 'the Singularity' advocate a similar vision.)

Today more than ever, we should leave this notion of global progress behind and insist on its localized character. A sign of genuine progress is, paradoxically enough, our becoming aware of this localization, of the embeddedness of progress in the system which it is actively evolving. This means that we also become aware of the multiplicities, the complexities and – inevitably – the inconsistencies of what presents itself as progress.

Consider an apparently minor phenomenon which compels us to redefine the predominant notion of progress. In July 2024, the media reported on a growing number of Chinese workers swapping high-pressure office jobs for flexible blue-collar work. Li, 27, from Wuhan said:

> I like cleaning up. As living standards improve (across the country), the demand for housekeeping services is also surging with an ever-expanding market. The change it brings is that my head no longer feels dizzy. I feel less mental pressure. And I am full of energy every day.[6]

This flies in the face of several major assumptions about what constitutes 'progress', including the idea that having an office job is more desirable, prestigious and lucrative than blue-collar work, and that this is a small price to pay for long hours and high pressure. So is this trend a sign of progress? And if it is, how should we redefine our notion of progress? Should we leave behind standard topics like pay inequality and gender representation in social life and shift the focus on to personal, individual satisfaction? Or would we, by doing so, be engaging in precisely the type of retreat from the possibility of political participation, political change which I discussed above as the culturalization of politics? We must recognize that progress is never a linear approximation to some pre-existing goal since every step forward that deserves the name 'progress' implies a radical redefinition of the very notion of progress – progress needs to be constantly redefined, and this redefinition is a crucial part of progress.

True progress thus occurs in two steps: first, we make a step towards actualizing what we consider progress, and when we become aware of the squashed bird that was the victim of this progress, we then accordingly redefine our notion of progress. It is in this sense that I define myself as a moderately-conservative communist: in order to survive we need a radical re-arrangement of our entire way of life towards some form of global solidarity and cooperation, but the urgent need to achieve this goal brings new dangers, so we should act with urgency *and* care.

An illusion is never simply an illusion: it is not enough to make the old Marxist point about the gap between the ideological appearance of the universal legal form and the particular interests that effectively sustain it – as is so common amongst '-correct' critics on the Left. The counter-argument that the form is never a 'mere' form, but involves a dynamic of its own which leaves traces in the materiality of social life, made by Jacques Rancière, is fully valid. After all, the 'formal freedom' of the bourgeois sets in motion the process of 'material' political demands and practices, from trade unions to feminist movements. Rancière rightly emphasizes the radical *ambiguity* of the Marxist notion of the gap between formal democracy with its discourse of the rights of man and political freedom and the economic reality of exploitation and domination. This gap between the 'appearance' of equality-freedom and the social reality of economic and cultural differences can either be interpreted in the standard symptomatic way – that is, that the form of universal rights, equality, freedom and democracy is just a necessary but illusory expression of its concrete social content, the universe of exploitation and class domination. Or it can be interpreted in the much more subversive sense of a tension in which the 'appearance' of *égaliberté* is precisely *not* a 'mere appearance' but has a power of its own. This power allows it to set in motion the process of the re-articulation of actual socio-economic relations by way of their progressive 'politicization': why shouldn't women also vote? Why shouldn't workplace conditions be of public political concern?, etc. If the bourgeois freedom is merely formal and doesn't disturb the true relations of power, why, then, didn't the Stalinist regime allow it? Why was it so afraid of it? In the opposition between form and content, the form possesses an autonomy of its own – one can almost say a content of its own. This content cannot be dismissed as merely covering the broken, bloody bodies within.

One of the reliable measures of authentic progress is a negative one: in true ethical progress, something previously perceived as more or less normal (slavery, direct oppression of women, torture) simply becomes impossible – if one tries to justify it, one appears as an eccentric idiot. The reverse is also true: when, as is the case today, the acceptability of torture again becomes a matter of public debate, we are for sure witnessing an ethical regression. Following a true progressive historical break, one simply cannot return to the past, one cannot go on as if nothing happened – if one does, the same practice acquires a radically changed meaning. Adorno deftly illustrated this point by using the example of Schoenberg's atonal revolution: after it took place, one could, of course, go on composing in the traditional tonal way (and one does), but the resulting music has lost its innocence, since it is already 'mediated' by the atonal break and thus functions as its negation. And the same goes for all domains: after the emergence of philosophical analysis of notions with Plato, mythical thought lost its immediacy, all revival of it is a fake; after the emergence of Christianity, all revivals of paganism are a nostalgic fake.

Last but not least, there are moments which we could call 'eternal' (falling in love, a supreme artistic achievement) where the idea of progress simply doesn't apply – moments which are absolute in themselves. There is a story that Italian composer Gioachino Rossini was asked who the greatest composer was; he responded, 'Beethoven.' When his interlocutor asked, 'But what about Mozart?', Rossini calmly quipped: 'Mozart is not the *best* composer, he is the *only* composer!' But there are also political events in which echoes of eternity interrupt temporal life. In his late 'Conflict of Faculties', Kant addresses a simple but difficult question: Was there true progress in history? (He meant ethical progress in terms of freedom, not just material developments.) Kant conceded that actual history is confused and allows for no clear proof of progress (think of how the twentieth century brought unprecedented democracy and welfare, but also the Holocaust and the gulag). He concluded that, although progress cannot be proven, we can discern signs that progress is possible. Kant interpreted the French Revolution as such a sign – a sign pointing towards the possibility of freedom. The hitherto unthinkable happened – a whole people fearlessly asserted their freedom and equality. For Kant, even more important than the – often bloody – reality of what went on in the streets of Paris was the enthusiasm that the events in France prompted in sympathetic observers around Europe:

> The recent Revolution of a people which is rich in spirit, may well either fail or succeed, accumulate misery and atrocity, it nevertheless arouses in the heart of all spectators (who are not themselves caught up in it) a taking of sides according to desires which borders on enthusiasm and which, since its very expression was not without danger, can only have been caused by a moral disposition within the human race.[7]

If it sounds all too easy to dismiss the bloodiness of reality, one should note that the enthusiasm generated by the French Revolution swept not only Europe, but also places like Haiti; and the enthusiasm there was not only that of dispassionate Kantian observers, but an engaged, practical one – a key moment of another world-historical event: enslaved Black people fighting for full participation in the emancipatory project of the French Revolution.

German Idealism disrupts the standard Aristotelian ontology which is structured around the vector running from possibility to actuality. In contrast to the idea that every possibility strives to fully actualize itself, one should conceive of 'progress' as a move of *restoring the dimension of potentiality to mere actuality*, of unearthing, in the very heart of actuality, a secret striving towards potentiality. Recall Walter Benjamin's notion of revolution as redemption-through-repetition of the past:[8] where the French Revolution, for example, is concerned, the task of a true Marxist historiography is not to describe events the way they really were (and to explain how these events generated the ideological illusions that accompanied them). The task is rather to unearth the hidden potentiality, the utopian emancipatory potentials, which were betrayed in the actuality of revolution and in its final outcome, the rise of utilitarian market capitalism. Equally, we could reconsider decolonization as an open-ended, ongoing experience which contains multitudes of possibility: the liberatory potential of African ways of being, organizing, living which are not constrained by the polarizing rigidities of 'Western' or 'African'. The point of Marx is not primarily to make fun of the wild hopes of the Jacobins' revolutionary enthusiasm, to point out how their high emancipatory rhetoric was just a means used by the historical 'cunning of reason' to establish the vulgar commercial capitalist reality; it is to explain how these betrayed radical-emancipatory potentials continue to 'insist' as a kind of historical spectres and to haunt the revolutionary memory, demanding their enactment, so that the later proletarian revolution should also redeem (put to rest) all these past ghosts. In short, a true progress also aims at retroactively redeeming all the squashed birds of the past progresses – not redeeming them in reality (the bio-cosmist dream), but redeeming the potentiality that was present in them.

Against Progress

Consider oxycodone.

The prescription pain medication, an opioid drug like morphine, codeine and methadone, was discovered in Germany in 1917. During World War II, it was widely used by the Nazis to keep their soldiers impervious to pain and suffering (Adolf Hitler's doctor Theodor Morrell gave it regularly to Hitler himself). Its most popular form was OxyContin (often referred to as 'Oxy'), developed in 1995 to provide long-lasting pain relief. Widely prescribed, OxyContin became associated with serious abuse and addiction problems. When the patent expired, similar products emerged onto the market with similarly destructive results.[1]

Consider Greece's Syriza party (the Coalition of the Radical Left—Progressive Alliance, to give it its full name), which on 24 September 2023 elected former Goldman Sachs trader Stefanos Kasselakis as its leader. Kasselakis, the son of a shipowner and CEO of a shipping company (with all the symbolic weight this carries in Greece), was until recently based in Miami. When he made his entry into politics, he was not shy about openly declaring that for him, politics was merely a stopgap between business ventures.

Consider BRICS, an acronym for the world's largest emerging markets. Many outside the developed West see the coalition of developing economies, which currently includes Brazil, Russia, India, China and South Africa (and is soon to be joined by Argentina, Egypt, Ethiopia, Iran, Saudi Arabia and the United Arab Emirates), as a sign of progress – not merely a new bloc to oppose the hegemonic Western bloc, but a new kind of economic alliance. A multiplicity of different cultures peacefully coexisting and collaborating for the benefit of the world. Consider the Russian foreign minister Sergey Lavrov's speech to the UN General

Assembly on 23 September 2023, in which he claimed that the efforts of Western countries to cling to their outsized influence over 'global affairs' was doomed:

> The rest of the planet is sick of it. They don't want to live under anybody's yoke any more ... Our future is being shaped by a struggle, a struggle between the global majority in favour of a fairer distribution of global benefits and civilized diversity and between the few who wield neocolonial methods of subjugation in order to maintain their domination which is slipping through their hands.

Consider pain. Consider the Left. Consider progress.

The technocratic dream that scientific advancement will alleviate human suffering produces the ideal capitalist commodity: effective, addictive, and productive of proliferating side effects. The Left 'modernizes' by eschewing 'old' battlegrounds like class struggle and social inequality. Valorizing anything which moves us away from the colonialism practised by the West leads to nations like Uganda (which just outlawed homosexuality), Iran (which just quashed a feminist rebellion), Afghanistan (with its continuing instability) and North Korea being celebrated as paradigms of anti-colonial 'civilized diversity'.

The worst thing that can happen to our concept of progress is to allow opponents of *authentic* betterment to define what counts as progress. Surely any affirmative notion of progress today should include finding ways to limit the free distribution of products like oxycodone; should include a Left which rejects the 'post-political' and aims to squarely address the gaping inequalities in society; should include societies which, whatever their flaws, leave space for self-criticism and internal critique. We should think like Hegel here: progress is never a linear approximation to some pre-existing goal since every step forwards that deserves the name 'progress' implies a radical redefinition of the very notion of progress. As Japanese philosopher Kohei Saito conclusively demonstrated in his ground-breaking contribution to eco-Marxism,[2] the only way to achieve real progress today is to problematize the very notion of progress which dominates not only our ideology but our actual lives. Yet, on a burning planet, even this does not go far enough.

The paradox is that one of the most radical ideas of authentic progress comes from an attempt to get rid of the 'progressist' aspect of Marx's theory. Unlike the 'modernized' Left who would like to leave communist notions behind, Saito's eco-Marxism envisions replacing the communist project of unrestrained growth with a different kind of Leftist thinking: 'degrowth communism'.

Saito's aim is neither to prevent the rise of capitalist modernity nor to combine it with conservative social values and practices (as different forms of fascism do) but to propose a radical alternative to the devastating ecological and social consequences of unlimited capitalist modernization. 'Degrowth communism' is really a misnomer, for Saito does not advocate a project of new austerity – 'degrowth' has a precise meaning here, that of rejecting the unconditional drive towards expanded progress that characterized even Marx:

> At a certain stage of development, the material productive forces of society come into conflict with the existing relations of production or – this merely expresses the same thing in legal terms – with the property relations within the framework of which they have operated hitherto. From forms of development of the productive forces these relations turn into their fetters. Then begins an era of social revolution. The changes in the economic foundation lead sooner or later to the transformation of the whole immense superstructure.[3]

And for Marx the same holds true for the transition from capitalism to communism – this shift becomes a necessity when capitalist relations become an obstacle for the further development of productive forces. In Saito's well-known reading of Marx, he demonstrates that from 1868 onwards Marx abandoned this progressist approach and focused more and more on how capitalism's ruthless exploitation of nature posed a threat to the very survival of humanity. He doesn't mince words here; Saito is well aware that ecological awareness has been co-opted by mainstream capitalist ideology to the point that (almost) everybody pays lip service to it. Which is why Saito's argument doesn't target climate-change deniers but the advocates of 'sustainable growth', the central organizing principle in global responses to climate change. Saito is particularly critical of the Sustainable Development Goals (SDGs), describing them as 'the new opium of the masses': in short, SDGs disavow the brutal fact that its goals cannot be achieved under a capitalist system.

Instead, Saito promotes his particular vision of degrowth, the slowing of economic activity through the democratic reform of labour and production: the transition to use-value economy, against affluence society; decarbonization through shorter working hours for a higher quality of life; opening up the production process towards more creativity and meaningfulness; the democratization of the work-process, so that the decisions will be left to customers who really need a product; the re-evaluation of essential work as opposed to bullshit jobs, so that tasks like caregiving become compensated in accordance with their importance.

Ecosocialist degrowth thus implies the elimination of some sectors of production (arms, advertising, etc.), radical reduction of other branches (individual automobiles, for example), but also the growth of some activities (education, healthcare, adequate housing, electrical and water infrastructure in the poorer areas or countries, etc.). Here, however, problems arise. An important critique from Rafael Bernabe claims that Saito embraces the vision of local cooperative and municipal initiatives as an alternative to capitalism and state centralism:

> It is hard to see how Saito's municipal socialism can paralyse the process of capitalist accumulation, nor is it clear how such local initiatives can provide a coherent alternative if the relations between them are structured through the market, in other words, lacking some form of centralized planning. Ecosocialism requires far more than cooperative or municipal initiatives: it demands democratically centralized planning.[4]

To achieve Saito's goal, strong, centralized and even, possibly, dictatorial measures would have to be taken. It is worth noting that some of these concepts are deeply rooted in Japanese history: did Japan not already enact a unique collective decision by isolating itself from the outside world and 'slowing down' in 1603, when the chaos of the Sengkoku period ended? The Edo or Tokugawa period, which began in 1603 and ended when the Meiji Restoration took place in 1868, was characterized by strict social order, isolationist foreign policies, a stable population, perpetual peace, and popular enjoyment of arts and culture. In spite of all the deeply problematic aspects of what took place in Japan in 1603, the Edo period provides a unique case study of how a society can be determined by a large, conscious political decision – a kind of collective decision-making needed today, more than ever.

So the paradox is that to effectively slow down we will have to mobilize in an as yet undefined way. Saito knows we need to rehabilitate planning, but this will have to be done in a much more brutal sense than he envisages. Just think about the global measures required to cope with global warming, population movements, and threatened or actual war, not to mention the increasing digital control over our daily lives. The next problem is that Saito seems to ignore how, with the latest trends, global capitalism itself is changing its basic structure to such an extent that it is doubtful if it should still be called capitalism – or if, to quote Yanis Varoufakis, '[c]apitalism is dead. Now we have something much worse.'[5] Indeed, Varoufakis considers this new epoch 'techno-feudalism'. So the question remains: Is the notion of capitalism on which Saito bases his critique still relevant in an age of techno-feudalism?

If progress, at least in part, can be defined as a continual resistance to fascism then a 'degrowth' model which relies on continual self-sacrifice and moderation and repressed desires can't be viewed as a form of progress. The agility of capitalism, its shape-shifting capacities, will always outrun this model. This brings us to the exceptional nature of capitalism. Todd MacGowan[6] provided a Lacanian explanation of the resiliency of capitalism, boldly admitting that, in some (very qualified) sense capitalism effectively does fit 'human nature'. In contrast to pre-modern social orders which obfuscate the paradox of human desire and presume that desire is structured in a straightforward teleological way (that humans strive towards some ultimate goal, be it happiness or another kind of material or spiritual fulfilment, and aim at finding peace and satisfaction in its achievement), capitalism is the first and only social order that incorporates into its functioning the basic paradox of human desire. This is why the imbalance of the system defines capitalism: capitalism can only thrive through its own constant self-undermining and revolutionizing.

The third problem is an even more basic one: is the vision of future society imagined by Saito desirable at all, desirable in the simple sense that the majority of people would find it satisfying? Do we really think pursuing a future which doesn't promise pleasure (or which specifically promises its absence, maybe) can really be included in a definition of progress most people would recognize?

Saito imagines a society in which desire is divested of its constitutive excess and is satisfied by its self-limitation, a society in which advertising and luxury consumer goods tend to be eliminated. In this he comes close to a position advocated by Buddhist economics. As its partisans repeat tirelessly, Buddhism does not advocate ascetic renunciation of worldly pleasures but the proper measured balance between wealth and poverty, between individualism and communal spirit. Indeed, wealth is considered good if it serves our collective well-being. The Buddhist notion of the right measure, of 'just the right amount', does not refer only to individuals: it aims at not harming oneself or others, where 'others' includes not only other human beings but all that lives. In contrast to Western individualism, Buddhism advocates a holistic approach: my well-being depends on the well-being of all others around me, but also on the balanced exchange with nature. No wonder, then, that Buddhist economics advocates a constrained/limited desire, a desire controlled by spirit, deprived of its excessive nature. In advocating this, it relies on a knowledge of the distinction between true desires and false desires. False desires are desires for pleasure attained through the consumption of sensual objects or through their possession, and they are by definition insatiable, bottomless appetites, always striving for more. True desires are characterized by their drive towards well-being, and to arrive at this state, a rational mind has to regulate and contain sensual desires. We thus arrive at an opposition between limitless sensual desires and the spiritual desire for well-being. As Buddhist economics advocate Ven. P. A. Payutto puts it:

> Consumption may satisfy sensual desires, but its true purpose is to provide well-being. For example, our body depends on food for nourishment. Consumption of food is thus a requirement

> for well-being. For most people, however, eating food is also a means to experience pleasure. If in consuming food one receives the experience of a delicious flavor, one is said to have satisfied one's desires.[7]

From my Lacanian standpoint, it is here that problems arise: what Buddhist economics aims at is a desire deprived of its excess, which is precisely what makes it a human desire! It is enjoyment deprived of its constitutive surplus. When we eat, we almost never do it just for our long-term spiritual and physical well-being: we do it mostly in a joyless way to satisfy our hunger, or we do it for the pleasure of eating, and it is this pleasure, not its subordination to some higher goal, which makes us human. However, this pleasure is never simply bodily, it cannot be reduced to satisfaction of a physical need. Our desire, even when it appears as a craving for some physical satisfaction, is always pervaded by an obscene spiritual dimension of a limitless expansion, which is why no physical object or act can pacify it. The opposition between false limitless desires which only bring suffering and the authentic spiritual desire for well-being thus appears problematic: sensual desires are in themselves moderate, constrained to their direct goals; they become infinite and self-destructive only when they are infected by a spiritual dimension. Friedrich Wilhelm Joseph Schelling knew that spirituality is self-destructive in its longing for infinity, which is why evil is much more spiritual than our sensual reality. In other words, the root of Evil is not our egotism but, on the contrary, a perverted self-destructive spirituality which can prompt unnecessary personal self-sacrifice. Think of *The Turn of the Screw*, where the governess's determination to 'save' the children in her care from the unholy evil of contaminating sensuality leads to one child's death – possibly, depending on one's reading of the text, a death literally caused by the governess's smothering love.

This dimension, of a destructive excess which is in itself spiritual, is missing in Buddhist economics, which is why its declared goal of the proper measure, when one attempts to practice it, tends to end up in some form of (not always) soft fascism. The basic feature of every fascist project is that of a conservative modernization: to engage in industrial and scientific modernization while keeping its destructive effects under check through a stable authoritarian power grounded in some traditional ideology. The paradox is that, because we desire the surplus that eludes every object, our very orientation towards pleasure and satisfaction compels us to permanently sacrifice available satisfactions on behalf of satisfactions to come – in capitalism, hedonism and asceticism coincide. Fascism tries to square this circle by way of containing it within a vision of society as an organic unity of its members. However, once we are in capitalism, there is no way back, which is why, instead of aiming at a return to some version of organic unity with nature, we have to do the exact opposite and denaturalize nature itself. Not only does being human involve a rupture between ourselves and nature, we should take a step further and admit that nature is in itself 'unnatural'. Nature is not a stable homeostatic system derailed by human hubris, it is full of self-destructive excesses and perturbances. The very idea of being able to move forward (let alone meaningfully address) the climate crisis is dependent upon a total reorientation of our sense of reality and our relationships to the phenomenological world.

The true source of our problems is not then, as Timothy Morton would have it, 'the most significant event to affect Western culture during recent centuries', namely the 'breakdown of the relationship between man and nature' and the retreat of the relation of confidence.[8] On the contrary: this very 'relationship of faith with reality itself'[9] is the main obstacle that prevents us from confronting the ecological crisis at its most radical. That is to say, with regard to the prospects of an ecological catastrophe, it is too short-sighted to attribute our disbelief in the catastrophe to the impregnation of our mind by scientific ideology which leads us to dismiss the sane concerns of our common reason, the gut instinct that tells us that something is fundamentally wrong with the scientific-technological attitude. The problem is much deeper, it resides in the unreliability of our common sense itself which, habituated as it is to our ordinary life-world, finds it difficult to truly accept that our everyday reality can be disrupted. Our attitude here is that of the fetishist split: 'I know very well (that global warming is a threat to the entire humanity), but nonetheless ... (I cannot really believe it). It is enough to look at the surroundings to which my mind is wired: the green grass and trees, the whistle of the wind, the rising of the sun

. . . can this really all be disturbed?' The difficult ethical task is thus to 'un-learn' the most basic coordinates of our immersion into our life-world: what once served as the recourse to Wisdom (the basic trust in the background coordinates of our world) is now the source of mortal danger.

Greta Thunberg was right when she claimed that politicians should listen to science – the line in Richard Wagner's *Parsifal*, '*Die Wunde schliest der Speer nur, der Sie schlug*' ('The wound can only be healed by the spear that made it') thus acquires a new actuality. Today's threats are not primarily external (earthquakes, asteroids hitting our planet) but self-generated by the human activity permeated by science (the ecological consequences of our industry, the psychic consequences of uncontrolled biogenetics, etc.), so that sciences are simultaneously (one of) the source(s) of risks and the sole medium we have to grasp and define the threats. Even if we blame the scientific-technological civilization for global warming, we need the same science not only to define the scope of the threat, but to perceive the threat in the first place.

What we do not need is a science that rediscovers its grounding in pre-modern wisdom, because traditional wisdom is precisely something that prevents us from perceiving the real threat of ecological catastrophes. Wisdom 'intuitively' tells us to trust Mother Nature, the nature which is the stable ground of our being – but it is precisely this stable ground which is undermined by modern science and technology. So we need a science that is decoupled from both poles, from the autonomous circuit of capital as well as from traditional wisdom, a science which could finally stand on its own.

Acceleration

Accelerationism, a recent form of historic determinism, is a notion whose basic core should not be confused with its different versions and aspects (neofeudalism against egalitarian democracy, abundancy communism, and so on). The impulse at the heart of accelerationism is clearly articulated by Nick Land in the title of his book on Georges Bataille, *The Thirst for Annihilation*.[1] Land's message is this: capitalism equals deterritorialization, a permanent intensification of development, a once-and-for-all overcoming of all stable forms of social life. In defiance of Gilles Deleuze and Félix Guattari, Land insists that there is no other effective deterritorialization: all attempts in this direction (especially the Leftist ones) got stuck and were consumed by capitalism. However, this accelerating process doesn't go on endlessly: a final moment is inscribed into its logic, the moment of the self-abolition or self-overcoming of humanity, when we will no longer be mortal humans confined to our bodies but realize our fantasies of becoming directly connected as one collective mind. As the title of Land's collected writings – *Fanged Noumena*[2] – indicates, the idea is that at this point, the Kantian distinction between phenomena (ordinary reality we experience) and noumena (the way things are in themselves) will break down and we will directly experience the noumenal Real. How is this to be achieved? One of the key foundations of this acceleration is the explosive development of Artificial Intelligence which will inevitably lead to the rise of the Singularity, a nightmarish/blissful Godlike collective self-awareness which will engulf individuals, depriving them of their singular selves, absorbing us into one glorious whole.

In the face of overwhelming humanist pessimism about what will become of us in the new world permeated by AI, accelerationism thus joyfully celebrates the self-extinction of humanity. However, this stance is far from asserting what Sigmund Freud called 'death-drive'; it rather amounts to its thorough denial. The headlong, exuberant rush towards a zero point is deterministic teleology at its worst: history has a preordained endpoint, and our gleeful push to reach it is joy at its purest. The Freudian death-drive, on the contrary, describes a process of endless procrastination, of missing the (final) point over and over again. As a close reading of Freud quickly demonstrates, the death-drive was the name he gave to a weird obscene immortality, a drive which insists on existence beyond the binary of life and death; what in horror is called undeath, the living dead. The accelerationist push towards self-annihilation is not actually a death-drive but simply a desire to reach the end. Like the shocked observers in *King Lear*, reacting to the sight of the slain Cordelia in her father's arms – 'Is this the promised end? / Or image of that horror?' – accelerationism posits that worse than annihilation is the perpetual postponement of that annihilation, the horrifying idea that the nadir might be endlessly deferred.

The term 'dark Enlightenment' used by Land[3] is fully justified: accelerationism brings the logic of incessant progress that characterizes the Enlightenment to its extreme endpoint. And the end that accelerationism desires is above all the end of politics as we know it: it imagines a society which will eradicate the social antagonisms that animate, that constitute, political life. (One should note here that Lenin too envisioned a society without politics: he wrote that Bolsheviks foresaw a future era in which social decisions would be made by depoliticized specialists.)

It is its naivety about process which makes accelerationism all too optimistic: before the post-political Singularity can be reached, we – humanity – have to confront much more immediate self-destructive possibilities, from ecological catastrophes and global war to social chaos, where politics at its most forceful will have to intervene. Even if this longed-for state of Singularity is achieved, it is immanently false: what it presents as a post-human future is a fantasy which remains rooted in our (human) finitude and mortality, its emergence is predicated upon us remaining finite mortal beings. To put it in speculative philosophical terms: humanity's historical existence is not the ultimate reality, it emerges out of a (pre-) ontological gap called by Martin Heidegger 'ontological difference', and by G.W.F. Hegel 'self-relating negativity'. Any vision of Singularity just avoids or obfuscates this gap, it doesn't really abolish or overcome it. Of course humanity can annihilate itself in many ways, but what will follow can't be anticipated. Hopes to the contrary are merely wishful thinking, wistful projections into that abyss.

The vision of the future described by accelerationism is more than a tendency. It is one of the 'superposed' determinations of our future which, to paraphrase Jean-Pierre Dupuy, if it happens will appear as having always been necessary. Dupuy's thinking is an important antidote to the too-simplistic view that there are two possibilities: catastrophe (whether military, ecological or social) or recovery. What we have instead are *two superposed necessities.*[4] In our predicament, it is *necessary* that there will be a global catastrophe; the logic of our entire history as a species demands it. And it is *necessary* that we act to prevent it, because the alternative is in a very literal sense unthinkable and because the dereliction involved in failing to act is unforgivable. In a collision of these two superposed necessities, only one of them will actualize itself, so that in either case our history will (have) be(en) necessary:

> There are no alternative possible futures since the future is necessary. Instead of exclusive disjunction there is a superposition of states. Both the escalation to extremes and the absence of one are part of a fixed future: it is because the former figures in it that deterrence has a chance to work; it is because the latter figures in it that the adversaries are not bound to destroy each other. Only the future, when it comes to pass, will tell.

Our ultimate horizon is what Dupuy calls the dystopian "fixed point", the zero point of nuclear war, ecological breakdown, global economic and social chaos, or some other currently unimaginable apocalypse. Even if it is indefinitely postponed, this zero point is the virtual 'attractor' towards which our reality, left to itself, tends. The only way to combat this future catastrophe is through acts which interrupt our passive drifting towards this 'fixed point'.[5] In an interview in September 2023, the retired Russian Major General Alexander Vladimirov described one such 'fixed point' when he warned that nuclear war was the 'inevitable' conclusion of Russia's invasion of Ukraine:

> 'For the transition to the use of weapons of mass destruction, only one thing is needed – a political decision by the Supreme Commander-in-Chief [Vladimir Putin]', the veteran commander warned in an interview with journalist Vladislav Shurygin. 'The goals of Russia and the goals of the West are their survival and historical eternity. And this means that in the name of this, all means of armed struggle available to them will be used, including such a tool as their nuclear weapons.... I am sure that nuclear weapons will be used in this war – inevitably, and from this neither we nor the enemy have anywhere to go.'[6]

A few months before this interview, Christopher Nolan's film *Oppenheimer* was released. Its use of the *Bhagavad Gita* during an intimate scene angered many Indian moviegoers, some of whom took to Twitter, wondering how the censorship board cleared the scene. A statement from the Save Culture Save India Foundation said:

> We do not know the motivation and logic behind this unnecessary scene [in the] life of a scientist. A scene in the movie shows a woman mak[ing] a man read Bhagwad Geeta aloud while getting over him and doing sexual intercourse'[7]

My reaction to this scene is exactly the opposite: *Bhagavad Gita* advocates a horrible ethics of military slaughter as an act of highest duty, so we should protest that a gentle act of passionate lovemaking is besmirched by a spiritualist obscenity. Is Vladimirov not doing something similar in the quoted passage? He presents a self-destructive murderous passion in terms of a higher 'historical eternity'. In order to find our way in the ongoing mess, we should follow the example (arguably) set by Nolan and bring out the horror which sustains the 'spiritualization' of carnal passion.

The caution issued by Vladimirov should absolutely not be dismissed as a mere strategic threat in the ongoing Ukrainian war: even if it was meant like that, it possesses its own remorseless logic which can push actors to actualize what they thought was only a threat. Clearly, we are already beyond the logic of MAD (mutually assured destruction) which prevented nuclear catastrophe during the

Cold War: mutual destruction is simply presented as inevitable since 'neither we nor the enemy have anywhere to go' … Key to understanding this seeming lack of recourse is Vladimirov's claim that 'the goals of Russia and the goals of the West are their survival and historical eternity' – what does the strange term 'historical eternity' mean here? It's a clue to the situation as understood by high-ranking Russian military personnel, as reliant on a series of radical choices: as if Russia, no less than Ukraine, is fighting for survival and thus neither has any way to de-escalate the situation. (Of course, this is wildly contrary to the facts as the rest of the world understands them: that Russia denies Ukraine's very identity and right to exist, while nobody expressed any intention to, or interest in, changing Russia's borders.) Russia is also fighting for survival only if we understand 'Russia' to mean something, literally, much larger: the geographical space occupied by imperial Russia, by the Soviet Union. This understanding is reminiscent of Anatoly Formenko's 'new chronology', which posits (among other things) that all the great cities and empires of history are mere conspiratorial refractions of Moscow and the 'Russian Horde'. What is eternal in 'historical eternity' is the enduring idea of Russia at its greatest, its most expansive. This is why Vladimirov doesn't invoke the excuse of Russia's justified defence against the Ukrainian attack; he even uses the expression 'Russia's invasion of Ukraine' – we are in the realm of manifest destiny, of the fates of great nations, of a battle to the death where such minor questions as 'who started it?' become insignificant. 'Let's not bicker and argue about who killed who', as Monty Python would have it.

So what is to be done? To begin with, one should read the situation closely to detect signs which may point in a direction different from the simplistic linear development towards doom. In mid-September 2023, it was reported that a human trafficking ring had been uncovered in Cuba which had 'aimed at recruiting Cubans to fight as mercenaries for Russia in its war in Ukraine'. The Cuban foreign ministry issued a statement announcing the discovery of the network and that authorities were working to 'neutralize and dismantle' it.[8] One should, of course, immediately ask the question: did Cuba, a tightly controlled country, really 'discover' such a ring so suddenly? They must have known about it for quite some time, so the real question becomes: Why did the Cuban government decide to make this 'discovery' public at this moment, and to end the network's activities? Does it mean that even Cuba, staunch supporter of Russia in its war against Ukraine, decided to distance itself from Russia's dangerous adventure?

More generally, the only possible principled and at the same time pragmatic approach is one of disavowal: to take cognizance of Russian nuclear threats but *ignore them* at the level of diplomacy and military strategy. The worst thing to do is to succumb to Russia's blackmail and follow the logic of 'we shouldn't provoke Russia too much' – one should continue to help Ukraine while making it clear that no one wants to appropriate any part of Russian territory (in its borders before the occupation of Crimea, of course). Russia should be pushed into a position in which it will be clear that, if it uses nuclear weapons, it did this of its own volition, not in desperate reaction to an existential threat to its territory.

And this brings us back to our starting point: accelerationism. Its basic weakness is that it is too static: the radical change it envisages is just the ultimate conclusion of one of the tendencies within the existing world order – in its very utopian vision of a post-human society, it utterly fails to interrogate the basic coordinates of this world order. We live in a strange time in which the scenario of a global nuclear war neutrally coexists with the culture war of populist neocons against Cancel Culture, while in the developed West life mostly appears to go on as usual – in the summer of 2023, people in Europe mostly worried about the possibility that bad weather and flight cancellations would ruin their holidays ... Our true madness resides in this peaceful coexistence of radically different options: it is possible we will all perish in a nuclear war, but what really annoys us is Cancel Culture or populist excesses, and ultimately we don't really care even about this but just about our daily lives. Rationally we know these three levels (not to mention ecological disasters) are interconnected, but we continue to act as if they are not. The only ethico-political imperative is thus a negative one: the plurality of today's crises makes it clear that things cannot go on the way they are now – how we proceed is a matter of risk and improvisations.

Holographic History

Are we living in a hologram? Originally proposed by Juan Malcadena in 1997, the idea that the universe itself is a hologram – that the three-dimensional reality which we inhabit is the projected image of something etched on an unimaginably distant two-dimensional surface – is by now familiar to theoretical physicists and consumers of popular science.[1] Could the political and social world that we currently inhabit be read the same way? Quantum mechanics defines a hologram as an image of an object which catches not only its actual state but also its interference pattern with other possibilities that were lost when the final state is actualized. Is this the way we live now, in an unbearably prolonged burst of crackling static as different futures teeter on the brink of collapse and consolidation? There is no longer one notion of progress which dominates our vision of past, present and future (even the usual mainstay headline of economic development is no longer convincing). We live in an era of the superposition of different universal visions of progress, each of them leading to a different inevitable future. The leading contenders seem to be: remnants of the Francis Fukuyama vision of the end of history; religious fundamentalism; and especially what I can only call a moderately-authoritarian soft fascism – the fusion of market capitalism with a strong state, mobilizing nationalist ideology to maintain social cohesion.

My suspicion is that this soft fascist option won't be effective against the threats we face today, and that a new form of communism will have to be invented. The ongoing geoengineering impasse makes the need for global cooperation brutally clear – it's the only way global warming can be addressed. The west coast of the US has been experiencing horrific prolonged heatwaves and the authorities' 'plan' is to spray gases above the sea near the coast, to block the heat from the sun rays from reaching the earth. Critics have pointed out that this spraying idea is risky not only because it may cause unpredictable damage in the area itself, but because it could shift atmospheric conditions elsewhere so that heat domes will just be displaced and re-emerge in other parts of the earth, most likely in Western Europe.[2] An example of how the effects of global warming can be redistributed (through wealth and power) – the rich countries will protect themselves at the expense of the poorer ones, 'outsourcing' life-threatening weather to them.

The climate catastrophe is *the* historical necessity that must surely push us towards global solidarity. However, history is not on our side (it tends towards our collective suicide). No wonder many commentators conclude that the battle against global warming *is already lost* – the moment has arrived for us to accept this fact and to rethink our entire strategy.

First, we should abandon the notion of historical progress. As Walter Benjamin wrote, our task today is not to push the train of historical progress onwards but to pull the emergency brake before we all end in post-capitalist barbarism. The complex interplay of catastrophe, potential and actualized, is uncontrollable and full of dangers, and such a risky situation makes our moment an eminently political one. The priority is to respond directly to our predicament: to prepare for the forthcoming state(s) of emergency which will become our new quotidian. The paradox is that acting like they will happen in all their dimensions (from ecological catastrophes to wars and digital breakdowns) is the only way we might prevent them *actually* happening. As Polish prime minister Donald Tusk said: 'I know it sounds devastating, especially to people of the younger generation, but we have to mentally get used to the arrival of a new era. The pre-war era.'[3] He is right, although not unconditionally – the situation is still in flux, and what we should say, to be more precise, is: 'If a new world war happens, it will be clear that it has begun back in 2022, with the Russian attack on Ukraine, and that its deployment was necessary.' Why this strange paradox of retroactivity? Maybe quantum mechanics offers a solution here.

While I am still learning about quantum mechanics, I find the insights it might provide about human history irresistible and one of them is that we can read it as 'holographic' – as the result of a series of contingent collapses of superposed possibilities. Such a conceptualization can provide an antidote to the teleological necessity which is too often elided into a narrative of universal progress.

Perhaps the supreme example of what we might call 'holographic history' is provided by none other than Karl Marx. Marx is not an evolutionist, he writes history 'top-down': his starting point is the contemporary global capitalist order, and from this position he reads the entire history of human society as a gradual approach to capitalism. This is not teleology: history is not guided by capitalism as its telos, but *once capitalism emerges*, it provides the key to the entirety of (pre)history: witness Marx's well-known narrative, as told in *Grundrisse*, of linear development from prehistorical societies through Asiatic despotism, antique slavery, and feudalism to capitalism. But there is no teleological necessity in this development; Marx does not claim that it *had* to be this way, or was always going to be this way.

Quantum waves describe 'the world at some kind of pre-existence level'[4] since what exists in – as – our reality is only the outcome of the collapse of quantum superpositions. At this pre-existence level, particles 'follow all possible paths when they move from one point to another'.[5] Consider the well-known double-slit experiment, in which 'individual electrons follow not one but every possible path from the gun to the screen. One path takes the electron through the left slit, another through the right, back out through the left, into a U-turn, and through the right slit once more.'[6] To understand how something emerges into our reality in a particular form, we have to understand that it enacted all possible forms, and that these 'superposed' forms continue to echo in the final form; like the hologram, it is indissolubly haunted by the unrealized possibilities it makes visible, the things it could have become, but did not.[7] Along these lines, Richard Feynman proposed the 'path integral formulation' which replaces the classical notion of a single, unique trajectory for a system with a sum, or functional integral, over an infinity of quantum-mechanically possible trajectories to compute a quantum amplitude. The 'path integral formulation' thus suggests that 'our reality is a sort of blending — a sum — of all imaginable possibilities'.[8]

When the wave function collapses, other possible superpositions do not simply disappear, they leave their traces etched in the single reality that emerges. Does something similar not hold for political struggles? When a peaceful negotiation wins over armed resistance, armed resistance is inscribed in the result. Media narratives like to remind us of two examples of the triumph of negotiation: the rise of the ANC to power in South Africa and the peaceful protests led by Martin Luther King in the US. In both cases, it is obvious that the (relative) victory of the peaceful negotiations came about because the establishment feared violent resistance (from the more radical wing of the ANC and key figures in the push for racial justice like Malcolm X). In short, negotiations succeeded because they were accompanied by the ominous threat of armed struggle; by the determination and commitment of those willing to fight, a violent conflict was inscribed as one of the futures hanging in the balance.

In *The Dawn of Everything*, David Graeber and David Wengrow propose that we abandon capitalism as the 'pinnacle', the outcome from which we reverse-engineer history to explain its creation and triumph.[9] Works like Graeber and Wengrow's project a kind of quantum superposition upon the actual early development of civilization. The Inca Empire, for example, was a big well-organized state which (for some time, at least) did not develop along the accepted lines of neolithic centralization, state authority and class distinctions. The split of Inca society into its 'anarchist' and authoritarian versions capture the moment when, in a kind of Darwinian struggle, two superposed social orders were fighting for predominance, and the authoritarian version won.

Along the same lines, some Marxist historians have pointed out that the explosion of capitalism in early modernity was conditioned by (the contingent interaction of) two unconnected factors: the availability of surplus financial wealth (mainly gold from Latin America), and the rise of dispossessed 'free' individuals through the privatization of commons. The surplus wealth was 'invested' and used to employ and exploit dispossessed workers. However, these factors were in no way predestined and history could have taken a very different turn, with the dispossessed poor enslaved or mobilized as a threat to the existing order and with the surplus of gold only bringing about its devaluation.

How right Jacques Lacan was when he pointed out that the idea of progressive evolution is a new form of teleology. The only way to break from teleology is adopting a top-down reading of history which conceives of linear progress as a retroactive fact, as the outcome of a backwards-projection of our standpoint into the past. In a quantum-holographic history, this retroactivity is rendered visible, and all superpositions that were present in the past and were erased through their collapse become apparent once again. In this sense one can even say that Walter Benjamin, in his 'Theses on the Philosophy of History', proposes a holographic notion of history in contrast to the predominant progressist-evolutionary version. A revolution in the present redeems the past in that it re-actualizes past superpositions lost in their collapse towards a ruling ideology. Such a direct contact between the present and the past is timeless in the sense that it bypasses the network of causality and temporality connecting the past and the present. As Benjamin put it:

> The past carries with it a temporal index by which it is referred to redemption. There is a secret agreement between past generations and the present one. Our coming was expected on earth.[10]

How can we read this claim without collapsing back into anthropocentric-teleological thinking? We go back to Marx and his top-down reading of history. In the introduction to *Grundrisse*, he wrote:

> Bourgeois society is the most developed and the most complex historic organization of production. The categories which express its relations, the comprehension of its structure, thereby also allows insights into the structure and the relations of production of all the vanished social formations out of whose ruins and elements it built itself up, whose partly still unconquered remnants are carried along within it, whose mere nuances have developed explicit significance within it, etc. Human anatomy contains a key to the anatomy of the ape. The intimations of higher development among the subordinate animal species, however, can be understood only after the higher development is already known.[11]

In short, to paraphrase Pierre Bayard,[12] what Marx is saying here is that the anatomy of the ape, although it was formed earlier in time than the anatomy of man, nonetheless in a way *plagiarizes by anticipation the anatomy of man*. There is no teleology here, the effect of teleology is strictly retroactive: *once capitalism is here* (emerging in a wholly contingent way), it provides the key for understanding all the other possible formations. Teleology resides precisely in evolutionary progressism where the key to the anatomy of man is the anatomy of ape. In a holographic, top-down history, the key to the anatomy of the ape is the anatomy of man which it anticipates.

This sense of radical contingency (brought about by awareness of the hologram images of what *could* have been) is also present in Kant. His writings claim that, in some sense, the world was created so that we can fight our moral struggles in it. So that when we are in the midst of an intense struggle which means everything to us, we experience it as if the whole world could collapse if we fail. A similar feeling occurs when we fear the failure of an intense love affair. There is no direct teleology here, our love encounter is the result of a contingent encounter, so it could easily also not have happened – but once it does happen, it decides how we experience the whole of reality. When Benjamin wrote that a big revolutionary battle decides not only the fate of the present but also of all past failed struggles, he mobilizes the same retroactive mechanism epitomized by religious claims that, in a crucial battle, not only the fate of mortals but the fate of God himself is decided.

Holography thus implies that the whole is a part of its part, i.e., that a part is composed of all the (other) parts of its whole. Capitalism is not only a part of history, a moment in the global narrative, it is itself the prism through which we see all the steps leading to it. True history is thus not a gradual development of parts, but a series of shifts in how its 'whole' itself is structured. We don't change past facts, we just locate them in a different symbolic context, we change their meaning. So, we do not have a whole which comprises its parts: each part comprises multiple universalities between which we will inevitably choose, without necessarily being aware of doing so.

Our predicament confronts us with the deadlock in the so-called 'society of choice'. In certain societies or cultures, we can apparently 'freely' decide about important matters. However, we find ourselves constantly in the position of having to decide about things that will fundamentally impact our lives, but without the knowledge required to make such decisions responsibly. Such a situation is properly frustrating: although we know that it all depends on us, we cannot ever predict the consequences of our acts – *we are not impotent, but, quite on the contrary, omnipotent, without being able to determine the scope of our powers*. While we cannot gain full mastery over our biosphere, it is unfortunately in our power to derail it, to disturb its balance so that it will run amok, swiping us away in the process. Whichever form our present morass of possibilities collapses into, it will remain inscribed with all the ways it could have been different. To remember contingency, to assume responsibility for the future in the full and painful consciousness of our limitations, is to think 'holographically'. And by doing so, we can remain hopeful, in despite of – because of – dwelling in daily intimacy with defeat.

Absolute Invariants

Albanian prime minister Edi Rama told the following joke at an international conference:

> Russia is considering unifying its time zones because there is a nine-hour difference between one side of the country and the other. In response, the Russian prime minister said to Vladimir Putin: 'There is a problem. My family was on vacation and I called them to say good night and it was morning and they were at the beach. I called Olaf Scholz to wish him a happy birthday, but he said they would be there the next day. I called Xi Jinping to wish him a Happy New Year, but he replied that they still had the old one . . .' Putin responded: 'Yes, it happened to me too. I called Yevgeny Prigozhin's family to express my condolences, but his plane has not taken off yet.'[1]

In this joke, Putin obviously thinks he lives in a universe where the future (of the bomb exploding on Prigozhin's plane) already exists now for him as the ultimate privileged observer. This brings us directly to our topic, the problem of simultaneity.

It is well known how special relativity theory relativizes the concept of the simultaneity of two events. As David Mermin commented: 'That no inherent meaning can be assigned to the simultaneity of distant events is the single most important lesson to be learned from relativity.'[2] The basic idea is clear: there is no absolute position in spacetime, every movement is a movement in relation to a certain observer and the position from which they are observing. The paradox this thesis involves is popularly described in terms of Albert Einstein's famous thought experiment in which a flash of light is given off at the centre of a moving train with one observer in the middle of the train and another in the middle of the platform. To the observer on the train, the light flashes reach the front and back of the train simultaneously; the observer on the platform sees an interval between them: 'For both observers, the speed at which the light traveled is constant, but the distance traveled (and thus the time consumed in covering the distance) varies depending on the relative motion of the observer.'[3]

Can we then decide if one observer is right and the other wrong? We certainly cannot prove that either is wrong: 'a simultaneity in one inertial frame need not be true outside that frame.'[4] Sabine Hossenfelder pulls out the ontological consequence of this paradox:

> [T]he physics of Einstein's special relativity does not allow us to constrain existence to merely a moment that we call 'now'. Once you agree that *anything* exists now elsewhere, even though you see it only later, you are forced to accept that *everything* in the universe exists now. This perplexing consequence of special relativity has been dubbed the *block universe* by physicists. In this block universe, the future, present, and past exist in the same way, it's just that we do not experience them in the same way.[5]

Let me also quote from Sean Carroll here:

> [F]or objects spatially distant from each other, there is no absolute simultaneity. A faraway event might be in the 'future' or in the 'past' of some nearby event, depending on one's frame of reference. The slightly slippier point is: therefore, if I want to attribute reality to all things 'now,' I have to attribute it to a set of faraway events that might be in the direct past or future of *each other*. And therefore I pretty much have to attribute reality to the whole four-dimensional universe, including events in my own past and future.[6]

The basic logic that underlies these conclusions is clear: we see the explosion of a star which took place millions of years ago now, so it exists now for us, but it existed millions of years ago for a putative observer who was near it when the explosion took place, so we have two nows, ours and the putative observer's. I see some problems with the conclusion that '*everything* in the universe exists now', the future, present and past. Can we also say that we – who observe the explosion in our now – fully exist in the future for the putative observer who was close to the star? What if a contingent event that might have happened a mere half-million years ago (measured in our time) were to annihilate all life on our earth? Would it not be more logical to say that everything fully exists in its own now (which cannot be synchronized with my own now)?

For an event to appear to multiple observers perceiving it in different nows, it has to 'really occur' at a moment simultaneous to an observer in the same place. Can we really collapse future events or objects into now? How can something appear 'now' to an observer when it didn't even take place? Only by reducing time, the temporal flow, to the limitation that pertains to our subjective perception – a conclusion which is also problematic! If the future also exists now, if (our) future events are real in the same sense (our) present events are, then space has priority over time – the future and the past would be real and present for an omnipotent observer able to see the entire block of past, present and future. However, what if time is not just another dimension of space but *a crack in space*, an imperfection of space which is not just epistemological but ontological? What if space *in itself*, not just as it appears in our limited perception, is imperfect and traversed by cracks?

Furthermore, what happens when we imagine faster-than-light travel (and information can travel faster than light when two particles are entangled, as recent experiments demonstrated)? We still have multiple observers, so it can't be the case that the eternal Now becomes reality and everything coexists simultaneously. So how will one observer perceive an object which moves faster than light for another observer? Since the speed of light is the maximum speed in our spacetime, the unavoidable conclusion might be that for the first observer, the object will move back in time. To go back to Mermin, the paradox of travelling back in time 'can occur in special relativity when faster-than-light travel is possible, because an object that moves faster than light for one observer can look as if it's going back in time for another observer'. Faster-than-light motion hence inevitably opens the door to causality paradoxes.[7]

Do we not encounter a somewhat similar spatial paradox when we consider that elementary particles, as we envision them, are both by definition microscopic and yet have a large internal volume? In other words, these quarks, leptons and bosons, like *Doctor Who*'s TARDIS, might be 'bigger on the inside': 'in general relativity we can curve our space-time so strongly that it'll form bags figures. These bags can have a small surface area – i.e., look small from the outside – but have a large volume inside.'[8] Like Mary Poppins' bag, these elementary constituents of our universe have the capacity to contain something much larger than should possibly be able to exist within them. Theorists of relativity tend to discuss thought experiments involving astronomical distances and mind-boggling paradoxes, but this disjunction between perceiving something from the outside and experiencing it from the inside is familiar to our everyday reality, too: a car appears from the outside too small for me to get in, but once I'm in I may feel quite comfortable in it. The problem could not get closer to home, it occurs within my own body: am I simultaneous with/to myself, my own body? The basic lesson of the analysis of perception is that I do not immediately see what I see: I rely on my expectations about the future to compose the mess of my perceptions and then I project this construct forwards into the now. In short, what I experience as something here-and-now is sustained by a complex backwards-and-forwards movement. As Hinze Hoogendorn puts it, what we feel to be the case – that we perceive events in our environment as they occur, in real time – is not just inaccurate, but neurobiologically impossible:

> ... at any given moment, instead of representing a single timepoint, perceptual mechanisms represent an entire timeline. On this timeline, predictive mechanisms predict ahead to compensate for delays in incoming sensory input, and reconstruction mechanisms retroactively revise perception when those predictions do not come true.[9]

So here we are (or were, or will be): unmoored in time and space, even within our own bodies. Nevertheless, amidst all this relativity, Einstein's special theory implies two absolutes. The first is familiar: that the speed of light is the maximum speed in our material universe, independent of the movement of objects and observers within this universe. The second is less known, but much more interesting: it is the existence of the absolute observable, the idea that the interval between two events can be formulated as a fact (a number) independent of all observers. However, the true paradox is that this 'fact' does not rely on the absence of any observer: each observer can arrive at the absolute interval not by ignoring his observations but by submitting them to the same mathematical procedure. Firstly, you take the time interval between the two events *as you perceive it* (and this interval is not the same as the interval perceived by another observer) and submit it to the prescribed procedure; then you take the spatial distance *as you perceive it* (and, again, this distance is not the same as the distance perceived by another observer) and square it; finally you subtract the two numbers and you get a number which is the same for all observers.[10] However, since I am not a specialist in relativity theory, rather than dwelling in the details of the absolute observable, I will shift to a homology which immediately struck me, a parallel with a key antagonism in our society: class struggle.

This resemblance begins with the thought that social classes are not an objective fact, they exist only as an effect of class struggle, which is why class difference is not a symbolic difference but the Real of an antagonism: it is real in the sense that it cannot be fully symbolized since it triggers two mutually exclusive symbolizations. As Lacan would have put it, there is no metalanguage in class struggle, no neutral way to describe it: *every description of class struggle is performed from a position within class struggle*. In other words, class struggle impacts the very notion of class struggle: it appears in a different way to those at the bottom, exploited, and to those at the top. To put it in simple terms, for those at the bottom, society is split into two antagonistic camps, while for those at the top, society is not split but a well-organized whole disturbed by extremists on both sides – a Right-winger automatically perceives himself as part of a moderate centre.

However, this 'relativization' does not imply a relativistic subjectivization: there is an 'absolute invariant' of class struggle, just as there is an absolute observable, and it too can be reached through subjective perceptions and stances. Indeed, a self-awareness of the position from which one is observing is an essential component of this equation. Of course, this 'absolute invariant' cannot be determined as a number; it can only be specified as a basic antagonism that is in this case arrived at by way of identifying it as the common denominator to which all class positions react.

The fact that class struggle logically precedes classes means not only that the relationship between classes is antagonistic (‘*il n'y a pas de rapport de classe*’, ‘there is no such thing as rapport between the classes’ as Lacan might have put it) but that the identity of each class is in itself antagonistic. The ruling class operates in a masculine mode, it is an exception which totalizes a society (which is why it perceives all other classes as a threat to social unity) – it is an exception in the well-known sense of an illegal element (such as unlawful violence) which sustains the rule of law. The exploited class is non-all (dispersed, not totalized) and for this reason it has no exception to sustain its unity – when such an exception emerges (as in the guise of the Stalinist Party), its ultimate outcome is the re-introduction of the logic of class power: seemingly seamless as space, but riddled with flaws and fissures nonetheless.

Worsting

I was reading Jacques Lacan's seminar . . . *or Worse*,[1] and was, from time to time, checking the depressing news from around the world: the continuing 'Russification' of Georgia (the imposition of the law on 'foreign agents'); Putin's 'peace proposal' to end the Ukrainian war (Ukraine has to withdraw from much of the territory it still holds); a renewed threat of Russia employing nuclear arms first if its existence is endangered (in Putin's interpretation, if Ukraine wins back some territory, Russia's survival *is* imperiled); the G7 meeting in Italy, where BRICS countries like Brazil and South Africa refuse to sign the joint declaration of support for Ukraine; our media full of the story of the eight IDF soldiers killed in Gaza, but silent on the question of how many Palestinians were 'found dead' during the IDF operation . . . With this cacophony of news in the background, a truly miraculous coincidence occurred. I stumbled upon a speech Marine le Pen gave after the victory of her Rassemblement National (National Rally) in European elections – and, like a lightning bolt, a link between this last news item and Lacan's seminar struck me.

The title of Lacan's seminar – . . . *or Worse* – immediately raises the question: What is the ellipsis standing in for? What is the missing term in relation to which something is worse? Lacan provides a hint when he plays on the (almost) homonymy (in French) between '*le père*' (father) and '*pire*' (worse). The full title is thus '*le père ou pire*' (the father or worse). 'Father' here is not just a reference to traditional paternal authority, but a variable, an empty spot that can be filled by different terms (that's why it is replaced by an ellipsis rather than the word itself). In sociopolitical terms, we can say that '. . .' stands for any social relation which implies a position of controlling authority: father, boss, leader, expert, professor ... Lacan's point is that when such an authority is gradually undermined, it tries to redeem itself by way of 'worsting itself',or, as he puts it in verbalizing the term '*pire*', '*ça s'oupire*', 'it makes itself or-worse'.

Are figures like Donald Trump not exemplary cases of the 'worsting' of a political leader, of a political culture of leaders? The (appearance of) dignified authority is replaced by an obscene paternal figure openly making fun of itself, resorting to dirty sexist jokes and racist innuendos. This populist Right is immanently 'popu-Lust' ('*Lust*' is German for pleasure); it allows you to indulge in your lowest racist and sexist pleasures brought about by humiliating the hated Other.

I cannot avoid mentioning here an unexpected homonymy of '*ça s'oupire*' (it makes itself worse, it moves towards or-worse) in my own (Slovene) language: the populist new Right '*se upira*', it (attempts to) *resist(s)* what it denounces as the new globalist elites which combine the deep state and the corporate powers.

It is also clear here that Lacan's point is not to issue a typical conservative warning against radical change, in the sense of 'If you try to undermine the paternal authority, things will only get worse.' Indeed, 'worsting' is precisely a desperate attempt to keep the old authority alive. This is why today's 'dignified' conservatives who want to return to the authentic forms of traditional authority (like Liz Cheney in the US) are condemned to fail – the only way out is a radical change of the entire structure of authority or, in this reading, the ellipsis.

This brings us back to Marine le Pen's speech after her electoral victory.[2] When le Pen took over from her father, her goal was, as she put it, the 'de-demonization of the National Front'. To make this strategy, or maybe the party itself, appear less abrasive, she excluded some party members accused of racism or anti-Semitism, and in 2015 she even expelled her own father. This is why the task of anti-fascists today is precisely to *re-demonize* le Pen: she is *worse* than her father because she largely succeeded in making her party acceptable to mainstream voters (in contrast to her father who remained a marginalized figure, seen as an extremist).

What is striking about her speech is its strict legalism, its emphasis on national unity. In contrast to Steve Bannon or even

Trump, she insists that her country already has good and adequate laws and that all her government (led by Jordan Bardella) will do is fully implement them. She claims it is the globalists in power who violate existing French laws, looking the other way when Muslim fundamentalists violate women's rights or react with intolerance at other cultures . . . Le Pen's supreme obscenity resides in the fact that she presents her extreme views as the embodiment of tolerant centrism, a bulkwark against all forms of extremism.

The new Right's agenda rotates around four central motifs: opposition to 'excessive' environmental worries, immigration and LGBTQ+ rights, and advocating a passionate patriotism. But many 'Muslim fundamentalists' (to use le Pen's term) are also against 'excessive' green activity or conservation, against LGBTQ+ rights, and against multiculturalists who undermine their ethnic or cultural identity. The conclusion that imposes itself is that the new Right populists are simpatico with the Muslim fundamentalists they claim to oppose.

This is clear hypocrisy. However, liberal multiculturalism – the common target of the new Right and Muslim fundamentalists – is also hypocritical, and not just in the sense that the multiculturalism of the West is not really open to others. The superego is at play here: the more supposedly open to others one is, the more guilt one experiences. What makes Western liberal Leftists hypocritical is precisely their fake self-critical stance which leads them to be constantly asserting their own guilt. It should be clear by now that 'worsting' is not solely a practice and prerogative of the Right. In this framing, we can read the endless guilty self-critique of the Western liberal Left as its own 'worsting', as it becomes the victim of its own hypocritical logic.

So how does the Left break out of this superegotistical cycle? Instead of constantly worrying about being accused of 'Eurocentrism', the task of the Left should be to rediscover the emancipatory potential of the European tradition – by re-engaging with it and rethinking it, if necessary – and to form alliances with Third World protest movements on this basis. So, for example, instead of justifying the obligatory covering of women as the expression of a culture different from ours, one should connect with the wave of women's protests following the death of Mahsa Amini which rocked Iran in 2022 – these protests didn't copy ineffective Western models of resistance, they were much more radical in targeting the basic power structure itself. What this means is that every authentic 'Eurocentrist' should fully support them as *more European than Europe itself* – in the same way that the Haitian Revolution of 1791–1804 was much closer to the authentic core of the French Revolution than the actual French Revolution itself.

So while we should expose the European tradition to merciless critique, we should also bear in mind that what enables us to criticize the racist and sexist aspects of the European legacy are the emancipatory elements of this legacy itself. We should also note that the non-European states which ferociously reject Eurocentrism tend to fully assume and practice the worst part of the European legacy, the notion of a strong nation-state (one need look no further than le Pen's 'patriotism' as an example). Is this not happening in today's China, in India, in Turkey, and many others? What goes on there is not a self-worsting of Europe but a self-worsting of these countries themselves, legitimized by European tradition. As for Europe, if what goes on now is a 'worsting of Europe' by itself, the only solution I see is a return to the roots of European thought – to Socrates.

The Socratic revolution is characterized by two features. First, it is a reaction to the general crisis of the Greek social life which, for Socrates, is embodied in the widespread popularity of sophists, performers of empty rhetorical tricks who enacted a self-worsting of the tradition of *polis*. Secondly, what Socrates opposes in this decay is not simply a return to the glorious past but a radical self-questioning. The basic tenet of Socrates' philosophy is the endless repetition of the formula: 'What, exactly, do you mean by [. . .]?' – by virtue, truth, goodness, and similar fundamental questions? Today, we need the same questioning: what do we mean by equality, freedom, human rights, the people, solidarity, emancipation, and all other notions we use to legitimize our decisions? The point is thus not to return to the legacy of Europe but to bring it back by way of rethinking it thoroughly.

Concrete Analysis of a Concrete Situation

Lenin died almost 100 years ago, and although he is a deeply problematic figure, one feature of his thinking seems more vital than ever today: what one may call Lenin's 'principled pragmatism'. Recall his well-known motto: 'concrete analysis of concrete situation.' This motto expresses the need to avoid the trap of dogmatic fidelity to a Cause, as well as that of unprincipled opportunism: in a specific, localized, fluid situation, the only way to be truly faithful to a principle – to remain 'orthodox' in the positive sense of the term – is to ruthlessly change one's own position in a new situation. In a properly Leninist way, G.K. Chesterton asserts that, far from being boring, humdrum and safe, the search for true orthodoxy is the most daring and perilous adventure – far more risky and much less passively opportunistic than the easy revisionist conclusion that the changed historical circumstances demand some 'new paradigm':

> Have we fallen into a foolish habit of speaking of orthodoxy as predictable and safe? There is nothing so perilous or so exciting as orthodoxy.[1]

Lenin himself resisted this trap when, in 1922, after winning the Civil War against all odds, the Bolsheviks had to retreat into NEP (the 'New Economic Policy', which allowed much wider scope for market economy and private property). His response was a short text, 'On Ascending a High Mountain', which uses the image of a climber making his first attempt to reach a new mountain peak who has to retreat back to the valley to describe what retreat means in a revolutionary process, and to explain how one retreats without opportunistically betraying one's fidelity to the Cause. After enumerating the achievements and the failures of the Soviet state, Lenin concludes:

> Communists who have no illusions, who do not give way to despondency, and who preserve their strength and flexibility 'to begin from the beginning' over and over again in approaching an extremely difficult task, are not doomed (and in all probability will not perish).[2]

An unlikely interlocutor we might bring in here is the Danish philosopher Søren Kierkegaard. For Kierkegaard, a revolutionary process is not a gradual progress, but a repetitive movement, a movement of *repeating the beginning* again and again. Is this not precisely where we are today? Is there any meaningful continuity with the Leftist 'victories' of the last two centuries or are we just starting from the beginning time and time again? Although sublime moments like the Jacobin climax of the French Revolution and the October Revolution will forever remain a key part of our memory, that story is over. Everything should be rethought, one should begin again from the zero point.

Starting from zero is crucial, especially now when it is global capitalism that behaves like a revolutionary force while the Left obsesses over protecting the achievements of the past (e.g. maintaining the welfare state). Just reflect on how much capitalism has changed the entire texture of our societies in the last few decades. One of the rare theorists and politicians who has courageously addressed the consequences of the recent shifts in global capitalism is Yanis Varoufakis who proposed a series of radical claims. One is that capitalism itself is morphing into techno-feudalism, which is why traditional anti-capitalist rhetoric is losing its efficiency – we should abandon social democracy and the central idea of a Left-liberal welfare state. In a properly Leninist way, Varoufakis assumes that the object of our critical analysis (capitalism) has changed, and we should change with it – if we don't, we are just helping capitalism to revitalize itself in a new form.

Such a stance is in no way limited to the Left – let's take a surprising example from Israel. Reacting to the ongoing deadlock of the war on Gaza, Ami Ayalon, a former leader of Shin Bet, demanded that Israel should enact a radical paradigm shift when he said, 'We Israelis will have security only when they, Palestinians, have hope.'[3] Ayalon went on to underline the point that Israel will not have security until Palestinians have their own state by calling for Israeli authorities to release Marwan Barghouti, jailed leader of the second intifada. Barghouti is effectively perceived by millions there as the Palestinian Mandela (he is imprisoned for over twenty years), and for Ayalon to call for his release in order to direct negotiations into creating a state for Palestinians is principled pragmatism in action:

> Look into the Palestinian polls. He is the only leader who can lead Palestinians to a state alongside Israel. First of all because he believes in the concept of two states, and secondly because he won his legitimacy by sitting in our jails.[4]

Let us conclude with an even more surprising example. At the end of January 2024, Ukrainian army chief Valerii Zaluzhnyi laid out a set of priorities for Ukraine and named challenges blighting the country's war effort in an opinion piece published after several media outlets reported that he could be dismissed from his post. 'The challenge for our armed forces cannot be underestimated,' he wrote:

> It is to create a completely new state system of technological rearmament. Crucially, it is these unmanned systems – such as drones – along with other types of advanced weapons, that provide the best way for Ukraine to avoid being drawn into a positional war, where we do not possess the advantage.[5]

I consider Zaluzhnyi's text a model Leninist intervention – and I am well aware that Zaluzhnyi himself and today's radical Leftists would consider this characterization crazy. I should also add that I am not qualified to judge the particulars of the power struggles which are destroying Ukraine and, indeed, Zaluzhnyi's role in these. All I claim is that Zaluzhnyi's text combines fidelity to the goal (maintaining Ukrainian independence and territorial integrity as a democratic state) with concrete analysis of the situation (how developments on the battlefield demand that the Ukrainian state and army should radically change). To put it bluntly, the heroic phase of popular resistance to the invader and close personal combat on frontlines is over. Ukraine should reorient itself to new technologies which imply war at a distance (drones, rockets, etc.).

Furthermore, Ukraine should assume the consequences of the international situation (the growing reluctance of the developed West to deliver help), plus it should enact changes in inner politics: more serious struggle against corruption and oligarchs, as well as a more open vision of what Ukraine is fighting for, a vision freed from any form of narrow nationalism and suspicion of the Ukrainian Left as pro-Russian. Zaluzhnyi was thus right, his advice is 'Leninist' in the authentic sense of the term. Only the changes he proposed can enable Ukraine to prevent the disastrous effects of the exhaustion of its own people from the war. Having the agility and courage to make these changes would be the most radical act of orthodoxy under fire imaginable.

Civil War

When Donald Trump was found guilty on all thirty-four felony charges by a Manhattan jury, he announced that he will remain a presidential candidate and that, if he wins, he is ready to act as president from prison. Even if this absurd scenario is disregarded (which it now has been), it's worth pausing to reflect upon the utter craziness of that situation, historical though it is: Trump is the first former or serving US president to be found guilty of a crime, as well as the first major-party nominee to become a convicted felon.

The fact that the Republican Party has nominated, as their electoral representative, a man tried and convicted of multiple crimes raises the stakes of this election well beyond the usual political consequences. Even those who are critical of the US state cannot deny that it is still perceived by many as the model of a rich and free society, attracting millions of immigrants. The spectacle of a presidential election in such disarray must surely elicit change in the global world order, and the spectre of an actual civil war in the US, once unthinkable, now seems not only frighteningly plausible but maybe even imminent.

How do we begin to approach such unprecedented times? We can begin by using a lens which enables us to see more clearly the underlying social trends blurred by the confusion of actual events: fiction, in this case Alex Garland's 2024 film *Civil War*.

The movie takes place in the middle of a civil war between a federal government led by a third-term president and multiple secessionist movements. The strongest, the 'Western Forces' (WF) led by Texas and California, ultimately occupy the White House and kill the president. The story is told from the perspective of a small group of journalists travelling from New York City to Washington D.C. to interview the besieged president, principal among them veteran war photographer Lee Smith (Kirsten Dunst), and aspiring young photojournalist Jessie Cullen (Cailee Spaeny). Jessie berates herself for being too scared to take photos; gradually her nerve and photography skills improve as she becomes desensitized to violence. When the duo enter the half-abandoned White House, Jessie steps into the line of gunfire while taking photos and Lee intercedes with fatal results. Jessie captures Lee's death as she pushes her to safety, and then, apparently unaffected, continues into the Oval Office where a group of WF soldiers are getting ready to kill the president. Jessie proceeds to photograph the presidential murder and the soldiers posing with their feet on his corpse.

As soon as I saw the film two reproaches emerged: first, *Civil War* can be read as an example of the *Bildungsroman* literary genre, which depicts the ethical maturation of a person who begins the story naive and confused; Jessie initially feels too much compassion for those suffering to focus, as the desensitized Lee does, on the job of taking photos, but by the end she is detatched and neutral, even capturing an image of Lee's futile, fatal attempt to protect her. Having Lee's engagement result in her death, while Jessie is the one who reaches the Oval Office and documents what is happening there, can be interpreted as suggesting that adopting the desensitized distance of the observer is the price that must be paid for the all-important work of capturing the truth of violence and conflict. But Lee's sacrifice subverts this valuation of 'objectivity', encoding within the film the idea that such neutral reporting is fake, a trap to be avoided at any price: today engagement is needed more than ever, because to be desensitized to violence means we already are part of a violent system. In Ukraine, in Gaza and the West Bank, and in hundreds of other places, only an engaged view, precisely one that prompts a response, is where we will find the truth we need to find. Was Garland aware of the falseness of this idolised neutrality? Probably not: he remains firmly entrenched in the ideology of neutral 'objective' reporting. But the tension he ignores is inscribed into the story, making *Civil War* a work which reveals/ exposes more than the author intended it to say.

The second reproach concerns a feature noted by many of the film's critics: the political divisions that propel the civil war are totally muddy. The military alliance between liberal California and conservative Texas is a patent absurdity, the authoritarian third-term president combines features of a Biden liberal and of a Trump populist and, apart from some casually racist remarks, it's not clear who the soldiers that the journalists meet on their way to Washington are fighting for. It would be wrong to dismiss this simply as a commercial strategy, intended to avoid alienating viewers who would might be opposed to a particular political position. As in the case of the film's praise of neutral reporting, the message that comes through is unintended, but for this reason all the more true. What remains and stands out when we ignore concrete political disagreements is the prospect of a civil war which has haunted American public life in the last decade or so, a conflict rooted in the growing disintegration of a shared social substance.

This dissolution is more and more the reality in which we live, and not just in the US. Yes, we have the big, 'classic' opposition between the liberal centre and the populist Right, plus some elements of a new Left (student protests). But we're also having to contend with a series of strange diagonal alliances (extreme Left and extreme Right both oppose supporting Ukraine), and a succession of new splits (the pro-Palestinian Left divided between peaceniks opposed to terror and those who support Hamas as an authentic resistance group that should be exempted from criticism).

My premise is that all these conflicts are pseudo-conflicts: even if they are very dangerous and may take the lives of millions, they are all attempts to avoid or obfuscate the true antagonisms that befall our global capitalist society, just as in *Civil War* the reasons for the violence are ultimately far less important than the spectacle of it. Trump's populism is, at least in part, a reaction to the failure of the liberal-democratic welfare state, so while we can and should support some measures advocated by the liberal centre (pro-abortion laws, racial equality, etc.), we should always bear in mind that in the long term, the liberal centre is at the root of our crises. This brings us to the well-known Antonio Gramsci remark from his *Prison Notebooks*: 'The crisis consists precisely in the fact that the old is dying and the new cannot be born; in this interregnum a great variety of morbid symptoms appear.'[1] The battles we are fighting today, from the populist Right to cancel culture, are mostly such morbid symptoms of the liberal centre.

Various reactions are possible to this mess we're in. Recall Sydney Lumet's 1973 film *Serpico* in which the hero is not simply an honest policeman fighting police corruption. His basic stance is a more subtle one: he just wants to stay out of the circle of corruption, refusing to accept his share of money offered by his colleagues, and he even asks repeatedly to be transferred back onto the street as a plain uniform policeman where corruption – at an institutional level at least – is mostly absent. I don't underestimate such a stance: by way of ignoring corruption, by acting as if the system functions normally, he becomes an even stronger thorn in the heel of the corrupted policemen than those who openly fight corruption.

However, in a situation where civil war looms on the horizon, the heroic moral stance adopted by Serpico loses its efficacy. Do we find this stance anywhere in the film? Is Serpico the small town in *Civil War* where journalists briefly stop to buy provisions, where people pretend that life goes on as normal, the stores selling fashionable clothes open for business? (On the roofs, of course, we see gunmen protecting the town.) Many voters behave in this way: they just want to survive the political storm in their safe haven, continuing their daily life as if nothing big is going on.

But when the state itself and its organs are directly implicated in crime, the *Serpico* strategy no longer works. Keeping your head down and pretending corruption doesn't exist only works if the larger social contract retains some force and integrity. Recall the scandal with Jacob Zuma, the ex-president of South Africa: after he was condemned to a prison term, he simply ignored the summons to go, and the state authorities weren't prepared to arrest him. The Western media were aghast at the inefficiency of the rule of law in a 'Third World country'. But how then do we judge a country where there seemed to be a serious possibility of a convicted felon being elected president, even doing his job from jail? And what if the mere possibility of this happening renders visible the half-concealed *truth* of our – call it global neofeudal or neo-Fascist – system?

Immediately after he left the courtroom, Trump said: 'The real verdict is going to be [on] 5 November, by the people.' It's clear what he meant – to quote the pollster Doug Schoen: 'While it's not a great thing to be convicted of a crime, what voters will be thinking about in November is inflation, the southern border, competition with China and Russia and the money that is being spent on Israel and Ukraine.'[2] Describing being convicted of a crime as 'not . . . great' is true enough, if a mammoth understatement; but such a conviction does make you a criminal, and it *is* a greatly unacceptable thing when a criminal can be elected the president of what is still the strongest state in the world.

Schoen's point is, of course, the negligent impact Trump's conviction might have upon his standing with the voters, and in this respect, both outcomes are catastrophic. If Trump wins, it means the end of the rule of law as we understand it, including the separation of powers. Trump has already announced the radical measures he will impose if he wins, and if he does win, the mere fact of his victory would imply the possibility that he could push through measures which will limit freedoms to such an extent that our common notion of democracy will become ridiculously inadequate to describe social life, without even mentioning international consequences (no support for Ukraine but full support of Israel, etc.) which will de facto amount to the US becoming another BRICS state. If Trump loses, it might be even worse: a large tranche of America will perceive itself as excluded from the public space – they will be pushed towards civil war and secessionist tendencies will explode since federal state power will not be accepted as legitimate (nearly 70 per cent of Republican and Republican-leaning independent voters do not consider Biden a legitimate President).[3] There is no middle way, no compromise between the two options in view (Trump's populism and Biden's legalist liberal democracy) – one can even question whether all-out civil war can be endlessly postponed.

So what hope is there? As Franz Kafka wrote in a letter to Max Brod: 'There is infinite hope – just not for us.'[4] An ambiguous statement which can also mean: not for us *as we are now*, so we have to change radically, to be reborn. Kafka also noted, apropos the October Revolution: 'The decisive moment in human development is everlasting. For this reason the revolutionary movements of intellect/spirit that declare everything before them to be null and void are in the right, for nothing has yet happened.'[5]

Today, the fact that nothing has yet happened means that all the main pathways to progress – the populism of the new Right, the compromised liberal centre, the old social-democratic welfare state, religious fundamentalism, even the naive belief that the strengthening of the BRICS powers will usher in a new multi-centric world – lead nowhere. All our futures are stillborn. The true utopia is the idea that a new world order able to cope with our crises, from the decaying environment to global war, will gradually emerge from the options that are available today. But this will not just happen without our intervention and engagement. What Theodor Adorno wrote decades ago – 'Nothing but despair can save us'[6] – is today more true than ever. This doesn't mean that we should just sit back and hope: we should act in all possible ways even without hope.

Authority

A lot has been written lately about the crisis of authority, as well as about the figures supplanting its failure: pseudo-neutral experts, populist demagogues, obscene clowns, murderous fundamentalist dictators . . . The first thing to understand is that this is nothing new: from the beginning of modernity, authority has been in crisis because a new authority grounded in competences and/or enlightened popularism will never quite work. Although conservative critics, from Edmund Burke onwards, who have been warning that a disintegration of traditional authorities will spawn much more brutal forms of oppression were wrong on the whole, there were strands of truth therein. This is why the next step should be to analyse the multiple facets and internal tensions already at work within precisely the traditional forms of authority for which many people long. And what better starting point for this analysis than Søren Kierkegaard and his sensitive remarks on the forms and justifications of authority.

Kierkegaard's aim was to reaffirm the Christian attitude in its 'scandalous' original form, before it settled down into a force of law and order (i.e., to reaffirm it as an act, as was the very appearance of Christ in the eyes of the keepers of the old law, before Christ was 'Christianized', made part of the new law of Christian tradition). This scandalous 'suspension of the Ethical' (of the old Jewish law) inherent to the Christian attitude is what Kierkegaard wanted to resuscitate in his furious polemics against institutionalized Christianity ('Christendom') that occupied the last years of his life. Kierkegaard insisted that every believer must 'repeat' Christ's scandal: every believer has to pass through Christianity in its 'becoming', before it turned into an established necessity. Recall G.K. Chesterton's perspicacious remark that 'civilization itself is the most sensational of departures and the most romantic of rebellions'[1]

– to paraphrase Chesterton, when a true Christian believer stands alone, fearless amid the knives and fists of the servants of established necessity, it serves to remind us that it is the agent of belief who is the original and subversive figure, while the mob of detractors are merely placid old cosmic conservatives, happy in the immemorial respectability of apes and wolves. Or, to paraphrase Bertolt Brecht from his *Threepenny Opera*, we enter the religious when we say to ourselves,

> What is a transgression of the law against the transgression that pertains to the law itself? What are the petty human crimes against the voice of God ordering Abraham the senseless sacrifice of his son? Which human crime can approach the cruelty of God's trifling with human destiny?[2]

What one should not overlook here is the inherent link between this suspension of the Ethical and Kierkegaard's notion of authority. In *Fear and Trembling*, Kierkegaard's Abraham attests his unconditional submission to God's authority through his readiness to sacrifice his beloved son. If he judged God's demand in relation to its content ('How can He demand of me something so atrocious?'), God's authority would be submitted to his human judgement and thereby devalorized. In other words, God's proper authority is experienced only in the suspension of the Ethical – in what Kierkegaard considers the 'religious'. If God were to be reduced to human ethical concerns, he would lose his proper authority and function as an aesthetic supplement to ethics – a kind of imaginary creature asking ordinary people, enslaved to imagination, to obey the abstract ethical imperatives. The religious suspension of the Ethical is not simply the external abolition of the Ethical, it is what makes it possible for the Ethical to exist and confers its identity, its inherent condition of possibility. This can also be understood in terms of the universal and its constitutive exception: the religious suspension of the Ethical refers to an exception which does not relate to the universal as its external transgression but, precisely qua exception, founds it:

> The rigorous and determinate exception who although he is in conflict with the universal still is an offshoot of it, sustains himself.

> The exception who thinks the universal in that he thinks himself through; he explains the universal in that he explains himself. Consequently, the exception explains the universal and himself, and if one really wants to study the universal, one only needs to look around for a legitimate exception. The legitimate exception is reconciled in the universal.[3]

At the very point at which Kierkegaard most violently opposes the alleged Hegelian 'tyranny of the Universal', he is, of course, at his closest to Hegel. What is the Hegelian 'concrete Universal' if not the 'exception reconciled in the Universal', i.e., the unity of the abstract Universal with its constitutive exception? The best-known example of this type of Hegelian thinking is, of course, that of the state as a rational totality of individuals who 'made' themselves by means of their labour: the state achieves its actuality in the person of the monarch who is in his very nature what he is in his symbolic determination (one becomes king by birth, not by one's merits). The exception of the king is therefore an exception 'reconciled in the Universal' since it founds it. Abstract, pre-religious ethical republicanism à la Fichte would of course protest against this royal exception, condemning it as an unbearable affront to republican principles and calling upon us to treat the King the same way we treat other citizens, whereas the Hegelian speculation demonstrates how ethical universality, in order to sustain itself, requires an exception, a point at which it is suspended.

To avoid becoming mired in such commonplaces, let us refer to an entirely different domain: the stylistic pecularities of Theodor W. Adorno. As Fredric Jameson pointed out, the rhythm of Adorno's essays always contains a sudden halt; the refined dialectical analysis is abruptly cut off with a proposition which clearly recalls the good old Marxist invectives such as 'ideology of late capitalism', 'expression of the class position of big capital', etc.[4] From whence arises the necessity of such repeated lapses into 'vulgar sociologism'? Far from attesting to Adorno's theoretical weakness, they present the way a thought's constitutive limit is inscribed within the thought itself.

Crucially, these 'vulgar-sociological' references concern the level of *content*; they point towards the 'social content' of the interpreted phenomena. Dialectical analysis is, ultimately, analysis of form; it endeavours to dissolve the positivity of its object in the totality of its formal mediations. Within the standard 'poststructuralist' perspective, it would therefore seem that such 'vulgar' references denote the moment of 'closure', the moment when the given field is 'sutured' and blinds itself to its constitutive outside. However, Jameson's point is that it is precisely such 'vulgar-sociological' references which keep the field of the analysis of form open, which prevent the thought from falling into the trap of identity and mistaking its limited form of reflection for the unattainable form of thought as such. In other words, the function of the 'vulgar-sociological' reference is to represent within the notional content what eludes notion as such, namely the totality of its own form: in it, that which escapes reflection, the form of its own totality, acquires positive existence under the guise of its opposite. Is it necessary to point out how it is precisely here, where Adorno purports to break the closed circle of the Hegelian self-transparency of the notion, that he is most thoroughly Hegelian? More precisely, it is only here that he attains the proper level of the Hegelian speculative identity: what Hegel calls 'speculative identity' is precisely the identity of the form, of the totality of dialectical mediation which eludes the thought's grasp, with some unmediated bit of content referred to in the 'vulgar-sociological' gesture (or, in the case of the state, the identity of the state qua rational totality with the 'irrational' biological positivity of the king's body). The proper dialectical approach therefore includes its own suspension, a point of exception which is constitutive of the dialectical analysis.

Therein resides the infamous dialectical 'coincidence of the opposites': the pure form of dialectical mediation maintains its distance from the positive content it mediates only by means of its coincidence with the most inert, 'non-mediated' remainder of this content; and the Lacanian 'Real' ultimately denotes such a non-mediated leftover which serves as a support of the symbolic structure in its formal purity. Yet the paradox of identity resides in the fact that it is precisely through this remainder of the Real – through this supplementary remark which maintains its non-identity and openness – that the system (whether Hegelian state or Adorno's theoretical edifice) achieves its identity with itself.

As Hegel puts it, a state without the monarch at its head is not actually a state, and the same goes for Adorno's theory which, devoid of the 'vulgar-sociological' sallies, would remain a maze of disconnected associations.

Isn't the same paradox of identity at work in the way fantasy guarantees the coherence of a socio-ideological edifice? That is to say, 'fantasy' designates an element which 'sticks out', which cannot be integrated into the given symbolic structure, yet which, precisely as such, constitutes its identity. The psychoanalytic clinic detects its fundamental matrix in the so-called 'pre-genital' (anal) object: according to Freudian orthodoxy, the fixation on it prevents the emergence of the 'normal' (genital) sexual relationship; in Lacanian theory, however, as Jacques-Alain Miller puts it:

> [the] object is not what hinders the advent of the sexual relationship, as a kind of perspective error makes us believe. The object is on the contrary a filler, that which fills in the relationship which does not exist and bestows on it its fantasmatic consistency.[5]

Sexual relationship is in itself impossible, hindered, and the object does nothing but materialize this 'original' impossibility, this inherent hindrance; the 'perspective error' consists in conceiving of it as a stumbling block to the emergence of the 'full' sexual relationship – as if, without this troublesome intruder, the sexual relationship would be possible in its intact fullness. What we encounter here is the paradox of the sacrifice in its purest: the illusion of the sacrifice is that renunciation of the object will render accessible the intact whole. In the ideological field, this paradox finds its clearest articulation in the anti-Semitic concept of the Jew: the Nazi has to sacrifice the Jew in order to be able to maintain the illusion that it is only the 'Jewish plot' which prevents the establishment of the 'class relationship', of society as a harmonious, organic whole. Which is why, in the last pages of *Seminar XI*, Lacan is fully justified in designating the Holocaust as a sacrifice to the Other destined to bring reconciliation: is not the Jew the anal object par excellence, i.e., the partial object-stain which disturbs the harmony of the class relationship?[6] One is tempted, here, to paraphrase the above-quoted proposition:

> The Jew is not what hinders the advent of the class relationship, as the anti-Semitic perspective error makes us believe. The Jew is on the contrary a filler, that which fills in the relationship which does not exist and bestows on it its fantasmatic consistency.

In other words, what appears as the hindrance to society's full identity with itself is actually its positive condition: by transposing onto the Jew the role of the foreign body which introduces disintegration and antagonism into the social organism, the fantasy-image of society as consistent, harmonious whole is rendered possible.

What we have to be attentive to is the inherently authoritarian character of this feature, that is to say, the inherent link of identity with authority: the monarch performs his role as a figure of pure authority, as the one who, by means of his diktat and decision, cuts through the endless tangles of pros and cons. And do Adorno's 'vulgar-sociological' outbursts not perform the same authoritarian gesture of reference to the Marxist dogma which breaks the endless thread of dialectical argumentation? It is by no means accidental that tautologies – statements which purport to identify with their subject – are the clearest example of ascertaining authority: 'Law is law!', 'It is so because I say so!', etc. According to Lacan, Antigone's defence against Creon's accusations ultimately consists of precisely such an 'authoritarian' tautology: she does not counter Creon's arguments with her own, she does not oppose to Creon's law of *polis* the subterranean divine law protecting the right of the deceased, as Hegel wrongly assumed; she simply interrupts his flow of argumentation by insisting that 'It is so because it is so!', 'My brother is my brother!' . . .[7] The best way to illuminate the logic of her defence is perhaps to evoke Saul Kripke's notion of the 'rigid designator', of a signifier which designates the same object 'in all possible worlds', i.e., even if all of its positive properties were changed.[8] The 'rigid designator' thus fixes the real kernel of the designated object, what in it 'always returns to its place' (Lacan's definition of the real). In the case of Polynices, it designates his absolute individuality that remains the same beyond the changing properties that characterize his person (his good or evil deeds). The 'law' in the name of which Antigone insists on Polynices' right to burial is this law of the 'pure' signifier, preceding every other law that judges our deeds: it is the law of the Name which fixes our identity beyond the eternal flow of generation and corruption.

Identity becomes 'authoritarian' the moment we overlook, in a kind of illusory perspective, that it is nothing but the inscription of pure difference, of a lack. In this sense, authority is far from being a remnant of the pre-Enlightenment: it is inscribed in the very heart of the Enlightenment project. Not until the Enlightenment did the structure of authority come into sight as such, against the background of rational argumentation as the foundation of enlightened knowledge. It is a symptomatic fact that the first to render the outlines of 'pure' authority visible was precisely Kierkegaard, one of the great critics of Hegel.

The crucial text in which Kierkegaard delineates the break between the traditional and the 'modern' (i.e., for him, Christian) status of knowledge are his *Philosophical Fragments.*[9] At first sight, this text does not belong to philosophy but rather to an intermediate domain between philosophy proper and theology: it endeavours to distinguish the Christian religious position from the Socratic philosophical one. Yet its positioning 'outside of' philosophy is the same kind as that assumed by Plato's *Symposion*: it circumscribes the discourse's frame, i.e., the intersubjective constellation, the relationship towards the teacher, towards authority, which renders possible the philosophical (or Christian) discourse. In this sense, the *Fragments* are to be read as the repetition of Plato's *Symposion* (repetition in the precise meaning this term receives with Kierkegaard): their aim is to perform Plato's gesture in new circumstances, within the new status that knowledge acquired with the advent of Christianity.

Both texts, *Symposion* as well as *Philosophical Fragments*, are texts on the love and transference which form the basis of every relationship with the teacher qua 'subject supposed to know'. Kierkegaard's starting point is that all philosophy from Plato to Hegel is 'pagan', i.e., embedded in the pagan (pre-Christian) logic of knowledge and remembrance: our life as that of finite individuals by definition takes place in an aftermath, since all that really matters has always already happened; up till the Hegelian *Er-Innerung*, knowledge is therefore always conceived as a retrospective remembrance, an internalization of what was already dimly felt and sensed, a return to the 'timelessly past being' ('*das zeitlos gewesene Sein*', Hegel's definition of essence). True, the transient, finite subject attains eternal truth at some discrete instant in their life; once the subject enters the truth, however, this instant is abrogated, cast away like a useless ladder. Which is why Socrates is quite justified in comparing himself with a midwife: his job is to enable the subject to give birth to the knowledge already present in him, so the supreme recognition one can grant to Socrates is to say he was forgotten the moment we found ourselves face to face with truth.

With Christ, it is just the opposite: the Christian truth, while no less eternal than the Socratic one, is indelibly branded with an historical event, the moment of God's incarnation. Consequently, the object of Christian faith is not the teaching, but the teacher: a Christian believes in Christ as a person, not immediately in the content of his statements; Christ is not divine because He uttered such deep truths, His words are true because they were spoken by Him. The paradox of Christianity consists in this bond linking eternal truth to a singular historical event: I can know eternal truth only insofar as I believe that the miserable creature who walked around Palestine two thousand years ago was God.

Motifs which, according to the conventional wisdom of philosophy, define the post-Hegelian reversal – the affirmation of the event, of the instant, as opposed to the timeless, immovable truth; the priority of existence (of the fact that a thing exists) over essence (over what this thing is), etc. – acquire here their ultimate background. Within the Socratic perspective, the truth of a statement resides in its universal meaning, what is 'eternal' in it; as such, it is in no way affected by its position of enunciation, by the place from which it was enunciated. The Christian perspective, on the other hand, makes the truth of a statement dependent on the event of its enunciation: the ultimate guarantee of the truth of Christ's words is their utterer's authority, the fact that they were uttered by Christ, not the profundity of their content:

> When Christ says, 'There is an eternal life'; and when a theological student says, 'There is an eternal life'; both say the same thing, and there is no more deduction, development, profundity, or thoughtfulness in the first expression than in the second; both

> statements are, judged aesthetically, equally good. And yet there is an eternal qualitative difference between them! Christ, as God-Man, is in possession of the specific quality of authority.[10]

Kierkegaard develops this 'qualitative difference' apropos of the abyss that separates a 'genius' from an 'apostle': 'genius' represents the highest, purest manifestation of immanent human capacities (wisdom, creativity, and so forth), whereas an 'apostle' is sustained by a transcendent authority which a genius lacks. This abyss is best exemplified by the very case where it seems to disappear, namely the poetic exploitation of religious motifs: Richard Wagner, for example, used Christian motifs in *Parsifal* to invigorate his artistic vision; he thereby aestheticized them in the strict Kierkegaardian sense of the term, i.e., making use of them with their 'artistic efficacy' in mind. Religious rituals like the uncovering of the Grail fascinate us with their breathtaking beauty, yet their religious authority is suspended, bracketed.

If, however, the truth claim of a statement cannot be authorized by means of its inherent content, what is then the foundation of its authority? Here Kierkegaard is quite outspoken: the ultimate and only support of a statement of authority is its own act of enunciation:

> But now how can an Apostle prove that he has authority? If he could prove it physically, then he would not be an Apostle. He has no other proof than his own statement. That has to be so; for otherwise the believer's relationship to him would be direct instead of being paradoxical.[11]

When authority is backed up by an immediate physical compulsion, what we are dealing with is not authority proper (i.e., symbolic authority), but simply an agency of brute force: authority proper is at its most radical level always powerless, it is a certain 'call' which 'cannot effectively force us into anything', and yet, by a kind of inner compulsion, we feel obliged to follow it unconditionally. As such, authority is inherently paradoxical. As we have just seen, authority is vested in a certain statement insofar as the immanent value of its content is suspended; we obey a statement of authority because it has authority, not because its content is wise, profound, etc.:

> Authority is a specific quality which, coming from elsewhere, becomes qualitatively apparent when the content of the message or of the action is posited as indifferent. To be prepared to obey a government department if it can be clever is really to make a fool of it. To honor one's father because he is intelligent is impiety.[12]

Kierkegaard is seemingly unequivocal; the teacher is what matters, not the content of the teaching. Yet at the same time he also intimates the exact opposite: an apostle – a person in whom God's authority is vested – is reduced to his role of a carrier of some foreign message, totally abrogated as a person, and subordinated to the only thing that matters, the content of the message:

> Just as a man, sent into the town with a letter, has nothing to do with its contents, but has only to deliver it; just as a minister who is sent to a foreign court is not responsible for the content of the message, but has only to convey it correctly: so, too, an Apostle has really only to be faithful in his service, and to carry out his task. Therein lies the essence of an Apostle's life of selfsacrifice, even if he were never persecuted, in the fact that he is 'poor, yet making many rich.'[13]

An apostle therefore corresponds perfectly to the function of the signifying *Repraesentanz*; the invalidation of all 'pathological' features (his psychological propensities, etc.) makes out of him a pure representative whose clearest corollary is a diplomat:

> We mean by representatives what we understand when we use the phrase, for example, the representative of France. What do diplomats do when they address one another? They simply exercise, in relation to one another, that function of being pure representatives and, above all, their own signification must not intervene. When diplomats are addressing one another, they are supposed to represent something whose signification, while constantly changing, is, beyond their own persons, France, Britain, etc. In the very exchange of views, each must record only what the other transmits in his pure function as signifier, he must not take into account what the other is, qua presence, as a man who is likable to a greater or lesser degree. Inter-psychology is an impurity in this exchange. The term *Repraesentanz* is to be taken

> in this sense. The signifier has to be understood in this way, it is at the opposite pole from signification.[14]

Therein consists the paradox of authority: we obey a person in whom authority is vested irrespective of the content of his statements (authority ceases to be what it is the moment we make it dependent on the quality of its content), yet this person retains authority only insofar as he is reduced to a neutral carrier, bearer of some transcendent message. The apostle is set up in opposition to the genius, who produces work in which the abundance of the content expresses the inner wealth of its creator's personality. The same double suspension defines the supreme case of authority, that of Christ: in his *Philosophical Fragments*, Kierkegaard points out how it is not enough to know all the details of the teacher's (Christ's) life, all he has done and all his personal features, in order to be entitled to consider oneself his pupil; such a description of Christ's features and deeds, even if truly complete, still misses what makes Him an authority. Nor do those who leave Christ qua person out of it and concentrate on His teaching, endeavoring to grasp the meaning of every word he ever uttered, fare any better; this way, Christ is reduced to Socrates, to a mere middleman enabling us to access eternal truth. If, consequently, Christ's authority is contained neither in his personal qualities nor in the content of his teaching, in what does it reside? The only possible answer is that it resides in the empty space of intersection between the two sets, that of his personal features and that of his teaching, in the unfathomable X which is 'in Christ more than Himself' – in this intersection which corresponds exactly to what Lacan called objet *petit a*.

As is clear from the passage from Lacan's *Four Fundamental Concepts* discussed above, the paradox of this double suspension is

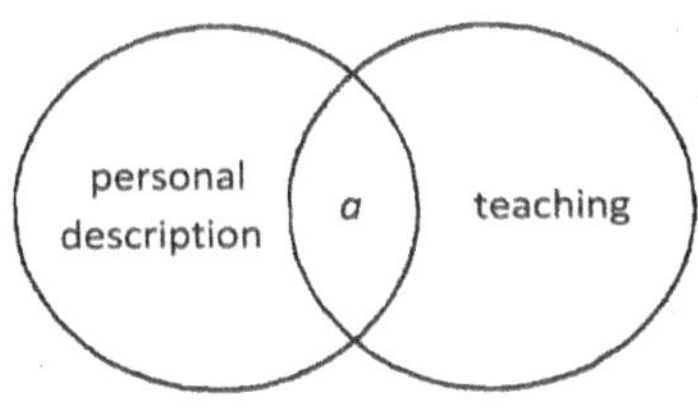

ultimately the paradox of the signifier itself. A signifier is by definition a pure representative which 'has nothing to do with its signified content, but has only to deliver it' (to conceive the meaning of the word 'fish', one has to obliterate all the immediate physical features of any particular species of fish). Such a statement requires its obverse, however, and that is the constitutive authority of the signifier: in the symbolic order, the purely formal network of differential features has priority over the content (the 'signified') of its individual components, i.e., its 'signified' is ultimately posited as secondary and indifferent. In terms of speech-act theory, this paradox is the 'impossible' point of intersection between constative and performative – the true stumbling block of this theory. Even in John Austin's *How to Do Things with Words*,[15] the evolution from the opposition of performative/constative to the triad of locution/illocution/perlocution and to the subsequent classification of illocutionary acts betrays a fundamental theoretical deadlock. Far from being a simple elaboration of the original insight into how one can 'do things with words', the transformation of performative into illocutionary act entails a certain radical loss: even at the level of an immediate, 'naive' approach, one cannot avoid the impression that, in the course of this passage, what was truly subversive in the notion of the performative somehow gets lost. On the other hand, it is clear that Austin was compelled to accomplish this shift from performative to illocutionary by the insufficiency of the performative/constative binary. The taxonomy of illocutionary acts proposed by John Searle[16] enables us to locate this lack by producing the point of intersection between Austin I and Austin II: one of the species of illocution ('declarations') coincides with the 'pure' performative.

The starting point of Searle's taxonomy is the 'direction of fit' between words and the world implied by the different species of speech acts: in the case of assertives, the direction of fit is words to world (when I say 'There is a table in the room next door', the condition of satisfaction of this proposition is that the content of the utterance corresponds to the designated state of things, i.e., that there really is a table in the room next door); in the case of directives, the direction of fit is world to words (when I say 'Shut the door!' the condition of satisfaction of this proposition is that the act in the world follows, realizes, the uttered command, i.e., that the addressee effectively shuts the door and that he does it because of my command and not for other reasons). The 'trickiest case', as Searle puts it, is, however, declarations: their direction of fit is double, world to words as well as words to world. Let us take the proposition 'The meeting is closed' – what does the speaker accomplish by pronouncing it? He brings about a new state of things in the world (the meeting closes – world to words), yet he accomplishes this by presenting this state of things as if it is already accomplished (the meeting *is* closed – words to world). He makes it happen by saying it has happened. In a declaration, the speaker

> is trying to cause something to be the case by representing it as being the case. [I]f he succeeds he will have changed the world by representing it as having been so changed.[17]

Every utterance, to be sure, accomplishes the act defined by the illocutionary force that pertains to it; there is, however, a crucial difference between declarations and, say, directives. By saying 'Shut the door!' I accomplish the act of command, but it remains for the addressee to carry it out and effectuate the new state of things, whereas by saying 'The meeting is closed', I effectively close the meeting. Only declarations contain this 'magical power' of effectuating their propositional content. The direction of fit (world to words) is not limited to the fact that a new state of things in the world has to follow the utterance, since the causality is, so to speak, immediate: utterance itself brings about the new state of things. Yet, as we have just seen, the price to be paid for this 'magic of the verb' is its 'repression': one closes the meeting by stating that it is closed, i.e., one pretends to be merely describing a state of affairs that already exists, disavowing one's own role in causing that state of affairs to (imminently) be. In order to be effective, the 'pure' performative (the speech act which brings about its own propositional content) has to endure an inner split and assume the form of its opposite, of a constative.

It is in the light of this split that one must interpret Searle's theory of 'indirect speech acts', i.e., propositions of the type 'Can you pass the salt?' where the primary illocutionary act (the directive, the demand to the addressee to pass the salt) is accomplished by means of a secondary illocutionary act (the interrogation concerning the addressee's ability to comply with the demand). Searle conceives such propositions as 'parasitic': their nature is secondary, they presuppose some logically prior illocutionary act (in the case of 'Can you pass the salt?', the direct command 'Pass the salt!'). Yet do 'declarations' not denote a case where the parasitic, in a way, came first, is original? Their primary illocutionary dimension (the 'magical power' to bring about the propositional content) can manifest itself only in the guise of the assertive, of a statement that 'it is (already) like that'. This paradox offers us a clue to Lacan's thesis according to which ontology pertains to the 'discourse of the Master': the (philosophical) discourse of being

> is simply being on thrust [*a la botte*], being on order, what will have been if you have understood what I have ordered you. The entire dimension of being is produced within the movement of the discourse of the Master, of the one who, uttering a signifier, expects from it what is one of its effects of link not to be neglected, namely that the signifier commands. The signifier is first of all imperative.[18]

The discourse of ontology is thus sustained by an 'indirect speech act': its assertive surface, its statement that the world 'is like that', conceals a performative dimension, i.e., ontology is constituted by the misrecognition of how its enunciation brings about its propositional content. The only way to account for this 'magical power' declarations possess is by having recourse to the Lacanian hypotheses of the 'big Other': Searle himself has a presentiment of it when he points out that 'it is only given such institutions as the church, the law, private property, the state and a special position of the speaker and hearer within these institutions'[19] that one can accomplish a declaration. In Hans Christian Andersen's 'The Emperor's New Clothes', all the world knows that the emperor has no clothes, and everybody knows that all the world knows it – why, then, does the simple public statement that 'the emperor has no clothes' blow up the entire established network of intersubjective relations? In other words: if everybody knew it, who did not know it? The Lacanian answer is, of course: the big Other (in the sense of the field of socially recognized knowledge). Declarations imply the same logic: the meeting is closed when, by means of the utterance, 'The meeting is closed', this fact comes to the big Other's knowledge.

When, in his *Four Fundamental Concepts*, Lacan specifies the Freudian 'primordial repression' as the 'fall of the binary signifier', he seems to allude precisely to this inherent split of the 'pure' performative (of the declaration), i.e., to the fact that it can actualize itself only under the guise of its opposite.[20] What is 'originally repressed', what, in accordance with a structural necessity, has to disappear in order that the symbolic network can establish itself, is a signifier of the 'pure' performative, i.e., of a performative which would not assume the form of its opposite, of a constative. In this split, in this impossibility of a 'pure' performative, the subject of the signifier emerges: his place is the void opened up by the fall of the 'impossible' binary signifier. That is to say, the gesture which constitutes the subject is the empty gesture of a forced choice: reality is 'subjectivized' when the subject posits as his free choice what is forced upon him, i.e., what he encounters as given, positive reality. This formal act of conversion of reality qua given into reality qua produced is founded precisely in the above-described coincidence of 'pure' performative with its opposite (constative): the performative production of reality necessarily assumes the form of stating that 'it is so'. Because of this split, the Lacanian mathem for the subject is $: an empty gesture of consenting to what is given as if to one's free choice.

The Lacanian S 1, the 'Master signifier' which represents the subject for other signifiers, is therefore the point of intersection between performative and constative, the point at which the 'pure' performative coincides with (assumes the form of) its opposite. We can see, now, what is lacking in Austin I (that of the 'performative') as well as in Austin II (that of the 'illocutionary force'): a kind of paradoxical, inward-inverted topological model where the extreme interior of the 'pure' performative coincides with the exterior of the constative. This uttermost point of intersection is of course that of authority; its immanent split is best rendered by the ambiguity of the verb 'to establish': authority is ultimately the name of a gesture which 'establishes (constitutes, creates)' a certain state of things in the very act of 'establishing (certifying, stating, ascertaining)' that 'things are thus'.[21]

Such an assertion of authority seems to be the very opposite of the Enlightenment whose fundamental aim is precisely to render truth independent of authority, in which truth is arrived at by means of the critical procedure which questions the *pro et contra* of a proposition irrespective of the authority that pertains to its place of enunciation. To undermine this supposed incompatibility between authority and Enlightenment, it's sufficient to remember how the two supreme achievements of the unmasking of ideological prejudices that grew out of the project of the Enlightenment, Marxism and psychoanalysis, both refer to the authority of their respective founders. Their structure is inherently 'authoritarian': since Marx and Freud each opened up a new theoretical field which sets the very criteria of veracity, their words cannot be put to the test the same way one is allowed to question the statements of their followers; if there is something to be refuted in their texts, these are simply statements which precede the 'epistemological break', i.e., which do not belong under the field opened up by the founder's discovery (Freud's writings prior to the discovery of the unconscious, for example). Their texts are thus to be read the way one should read the text of a dream, according to Lacan: as 'sacred' texts which are in a radical sense 'beyond criticism' since they constitute the very horizon of veracity.

For that reason, every 'further development' of Marxism or psychoanalysis necessarily assumes the form of a 'return' to Marx or Freud: a (re)discovery of some hitherto overlooked stratum of their work, of bringing to light what the founders 'produced without knowing what they produced', to invoke Louis Althusser's formula. In his article on Charlie Chaplin's *Limelight*, Andre Bazin recommends the same attitude as the only one which befits Chaplin's genius: even when some details in *Limelight* appear to us aborted and dull (the tedious first hour of the film; Calvero's pathetic vulgar-philosophical outbursts, etc.), we have to turn the critical scrutiny on ourselves and ask what was wrong with our approach to the film, our expectations of it.[22] Such an attitude clearly articulates the transferential relationship of the pupil to the teacher: the teacher is by definition 'supposed to know', the fault is always ours. The scandalous truth authenticated by the history of psychoanalysis and Marxism is that such a 'dogmatic' approach proves far more productive than 'open', critical dealing with the founder's text: how much more fecund was Lacan's 'dogmatic' return to Freud than the American academic machinery which transformed Freud's oeuvre into a collection of positive scientific hypotheses to be tested, refuted, combined, developed, and so on!

Lacan's scandal, the dimension of his work which resists incorporation into the academic machinery, ultimately resides in the fact that he openly and shamelessly posited himself as such an authority. He repeated the Kierkegaardian gesture in relationship to his followers: what he demanded of them was not fidelity to some general theoretical propositions, but precisely fidelity to his person – which is why the circular letter announcing the foundation of La Cause freudienne is addressed to 'those who love me'. This unbreakable link between the doctrine and the contingent person of the teacher, i.e., to the teacher qua material surplus that sticks out from the neutral edifice of knowledge, is the scandal everybody who considers theirselves Lacanian has to consider themself implicated in: Lacan was not a Socratic master obliterating himself before hard-won knowledge. His theory sustains itself only through the transferential relationship to its founder. In this precise sense, Marx, Freud and Lacan are not 'geniuses', but 'apostles': when somebody says, 'I follow Lacan because his reading of Freud is the most intelligent and persuasive', he immediately exposes himself as non-Lacanian.

This 'scandal', the blemish of contingent individuality upon the neutral field of knowledge, points towards what we could designate Kierkegaard's 'materialist reversal of Hegel'. Hegel ultimately stays within the boundary of the 'Socratic' universe: in his *Phenomenology of Spirit*, consciousness arrives at the Truth, recollects it and internalizes it, via its own effort, by comparing itself with its own immanent Notion, by confronting the positive content of its statements with its own place of enunciation, by working through its own split, without any external support or point of reference. The standpoint of dialectical truth (the 'for us') is not added to the consciousness as a kind of external standard by which the progress of that consciousness is then measured: 'we', dialecticians, are nothing but passive observers who retroactively reconstruct the way consciousness itself arrived at the Truth (i.e., the 'absolute' standpoint without presuppositions). When, at some point of the journey of consciousness, Truth effectively appears as a positive entity possessing an independent existence, as an 'in itself' assuming the role of the external measure of the consciousness's 'working through', this is simply a necessary self-deception 'sublated' in the further succession of the 'experiences of consciousness'. In other words – in the words of the relationship between belief and knowledge – the subject's belief in an (external) authority which is to be accepted unconditionally and 'irrationally' is nothing but a transitional stage 'sublated' by the passage into reflected knowledge. For Kierkegaard, on the contrary, our belief in the person of the Saviour is the absolute, un-abolishable condition of our access to truth: eternal truth itself clings to this contingent material externality and the moment we lose this little piece of the real (the historical fact of Incarnation), the moment we cut our link with this material fragment (reinterpreting it as a parable of man's affinity with God, for example), the entire edifice of Christian knowledge crumbles.

On another level, the same goes for psychoanalysis: in the psychoanalytic cure, there is no knowledge without the 'presence of the analyst', without the impact of his dumb material weight. Here we encounter the inherent limitation of all attempts to conceive of a psychoanalytic cure on the model of the Hegelian reflective movement in the course of which the subject becomes conscious of his own 'substantial' content, i.e., arrives at the repressed truth which dwells deep in him.[23] If such were the case, psychoanalysis would be the ultimate stage of the Socratic 'Know thyself!' and the psychoanalyst's role would be that of an *accoucheur*, a kind of 'vanishing mediator' enabling the subject to achieve communication with himself by finding access to its repressed traumas.

This dilemma presents itself most vividly apropos of the role of transference in the psychoanalytic cure. Insofar as we remain within the domain of the Socratic logic of remembrance, transference is not an 'effective' repetition but rather a means of recollection: the analysand 'projects' past traumas which unconsciously determine his present behaviour (repressed and unresolved conflicts with his father, for example) onto his relationship to the analyst; by means of the deft manipulation of the transferential situation, the analyst then enables the analysand to recall the traumas which were hitherto 'acted out' blindly. In other words, the task of the analyst is to make evident to the analysand how 'he (the analyst) is not really the father', i.e., to bring to awareness how the analysand, caught in the transference, used his relationship to the analyst to stage past traumas. Lacan's emphasis is, on the contrary, Kierkegaardian through and through: transferential repetition cannot be reduced to remembrance, and transference is not a kind of 'theatre of shadows' where we settle with past traumas *in effigia*. It is repetition in the full meaning of the term, i.e., in it, the past trauma is literally repeated, 'actualized'. The analyst is not the father's 'shadow', he is a presence in front of which the past battle has to be fought out 'for real'.

The point of the preceding argumentation, of course, is not to defend blind submission to authority, but to illuminate the fact that discourse itself is in its fundamental structure 'authoritarian' (for that reason, the 'discourse of the Master' is the first, 'founding' discourse in the Lacanian matrix of the four discourses; or, as Jacques Derrida would say in his late writings, every discursive field is founded on some 'violent' ethico-political decision). Out of the free-floating dispersion of signifiers, a consistent field of meaning emerges through the intervention of a Master Signifier, why? The answer is contained in the paradox of the 'finite infinity/totality' which, as one knows from Claude Levi-Strauss onwards, pertains to the very notion of the signifier: the symbolic order in which the subject is embedded is simultaneously 'finite' (it consists of a limited and ultimately contingent network which never overlaps with the Real) and 'infinite', or, to use a Sartrean term, 'totalizing' (in any given language, 'everything can be told', there is no external standpoint from which one can judge its limitations). Because of this inherent tension, every language contains a paradoxical element which, within its field, stands in for what eludes it – in Lacanese, in every set of signifiers, there is always 'at least one' which functions as the signifier of the very lack of the signifier. This signifier is the Master Signifier: the 'empty' signifier which totalizes ('quilts') the dispersed field – in it, the infinite chain of causes ('knowledge') is interrupted with a founding act of abyssal violence.

The philosophical term for this inversion of impotence into a constitutive power is, of course, the notion of the transcendental with all its inherent paradoxes: the subject experiences as his constitutive power the very horizon which frames his vision due to his finitude. For that reason, it is precisely the notion of the transcendental which enables us to distinguish Lacan from, say, Jürgen Habermas. With Habermas, the status of the 'disturbances' which vitiate the course of 'rational argumentation' by way of a non-reflected constraint is ultimately contingent/empirical; these 'disturbances' emerge as empirical impediments on the path to gradual realization of the transcendental regulative Idea. Whereas with Lacan, the status of the Master Signifier, the signifier of the symbolic authority founded only in itself (in its own act of enunciation), is strictly transcendental: the gesture which 'distorts' a symbolic field, which 'curves' its space by introducing in it an unfounded violence, is *stricto sensu* correlative to its very establishment. In other words, the moment we subtract from a discursive field its 'distortion', the field itself disintegrates ('dequilts'). Lacan's position is therefore the very opposite of that of Habermas, according to whom the inherent pragmatic presuppositions of a discourse are 'non-authoritarian' (the notion of discourse implies the idea of a communication free of constraint where only rational argumentation counts, etc.).

Lacan's fundamental thesis is that the Master is by definition an impostor. The Master is somebody who, upon finding himself at the site of the constitutive lack in the structure, acts as if he holds the reins of that surplus, of the mysterious X which eludes the grasp of the structure. This accounts for the difference between Habermas and Lacan as to the role of the Master: with Lacan, the Master is an impostor, yet the place he occupies – the site of the lack in the structure – cannot be abolished, since the very finitude of every discursive field imposes its structural necessity. The unmasking of the Master's imposture does not abolish the place he occupies, it just renders it visible in its original emptiness, i.e., as preceding the element which fills it out. Hence the Lacanian notion of the analyst as the obverse (*l'envers*) of the Master: of somebody who holds the place of the Master, yet who, by means of his (non)activity, undermines the Master's charisma, suspends the effect of 'quilting', and thus renders visible the distance that separates the Master from the place it occupies, i.e., the radical contingency of the subject who occupies this place.

Consequently, Lacan and Habermas's strategies of subverting symbolic authority are fundamentally different despite some seeming similarities. Habermas simply relies on the gradual reflective elucidation of the implicit prejudices which distort communication, i.e., on the asymptotic approach to the regulative ideal of free, unconstrained communication. Lacan is also anti-authoritarian, he is as far as possible from any kind of obscurantism of the ineffable, he too remains thoroughly attached to the space of public communication. This unexpected proximity of Lacan to Habermas is corroborated by a procedure, proposed by Lacan, which caused a great amount of resistance even among some of his closest followers: *la passe*, the 'passage' of an analysand into the place of the analyst. Its crux is the intermediate role of the so-called *passeurs*: the analysand (the *passant*) narrates the results of his analysis, the insights at which he arrived, to the two *passeurs*, his peers, who report on it to the committee (*comite de la passe*) – the committee then decides on the analysand's 'passage' to the place of the analyst. The idea of these two middlemen who channel every contact between the *passant* and the committee is very 'Habermasian' indeed: they are there to prevent any kind of initiatic relationship between the *passant* and the committee, i.e., to prevent *la passe* from functioning as the transmission of an initiatic knowledge, after the model of secret cults: the analysand must be able to formulate the results of his analysis in such a way that the two *passeurs*, these two average men who stand in for the common knowledge, are able to transmit it integrally to the committee – in other words, the detour through the field of public knowledge must not affect the 'message' in any way.

However, the contrast between Habermas and Lacan finds its clearest expression apropos of the notion of the 'ideal speech situation': Habermas conceives it as the asymptotic ideal of intersubjective communication free of constraint where the participants arrive at consensus by means of rational argumentation. Contrary to common opinion, Lacan also knows of an 'ideal speech situation' which undermines the imposture of the Master Signifier: it is none other than the analytic situation itself – here, the abyss that separates Lacan from Habermas is unmistakable. In the process of psychoanalysis, we also have two subjects speaking to each other; yet instead of facing each other and exchanging arguments, one of them lies on the couch, stares into thin air and throws out disconnected prattle, whereas the other mostly stays silent and terrorizes the first by the weight of his oppressive mute presence. This situation is 'free of constraint' in the precise meaning of suspending the structural role of the Master Signifier: the analytic discourse as the obverse of the discourse of the Master transposes us into a state of undecidability which precedes the 'quilting' of the discursive field by a Master Signifier, i.e., into the state of 'free-floating' signifiers – what is 'repeated' in it is ultimately the very contingency which engendered the analysand's symbolic space.

Although all of Kierkegaard's work seems to move in this direction, his actual statements are more refined – recall his claim about the futility of philosophical systems (his target here is, of course, Hegel):

> In relation to their systems most systematisers are like a man who builds an enormous castle and lives in a shack close by; they do not live in their own enormous systematic buildings.[24]

As is often the case in Kierkegaard's critique of Hegel, he misses the point and ignores his own proximity to Hegel: the final result of the Hegelian movement is precisely that enormous castles are only finished when they are accompanied/supplemented by a small shack in which the subject who built them has to dwell . . . In short, to paraphrase Hegel's well-known programmatic slogan from his *Phenomenology*: one should conceive the Absolute not only as a magnificent castle but also as a small shack attached to it. Or the Christian version: one should conceive God not only as the majestic creator of everything but also as a miserable individual walking around Palestine 2,000 years ago. In his *Castle*, Kafka has a clear premonition of this paradox: the novel's hero decides to climb up the hill and approaches the majestic castle on the top of it; however, the closer he comes to the castle, the more he notices that the castle is not composed of majestic buildings but dirty small shacks . . .

And exactly the same holds for language: there is no great castle of Language with all its noble poetic or scientific statements without what amounts to the linguistic version of small dirty shacks. As Lacan repeatedly points out, 'primordial' speech acts are single exclamations, as a rule curses or vulgar words ('Shit', 'Wow!' . . .), which play a very specific role: they are neither statements about things and processes that are going on in reality (like 'a storm is coming from the north'), nor are they expressions of our inner reaction to external events (fear, anger, joy . . .). At their most basic, they express our lack of a proper place in the symbolic order in which we dwell. We enter the symbolic order first as its objects: we somehow grasp that others are talking about us, that we are within the scope of their interest, but we don't clearly understand what they are saying, what they want from us, what they see in us – language as a medium is a big Other, connecting us with others and simultaneously walling us off, separating us, from them. It is in this sense, for Lacan (who often evokes his dog Justine), that dogs speak without really inhabiting language; they are unable to subjectivize themselves in it, to assume a stance towards others in it. They are perplexed by human language, and they get frustrated by their inability to participate in linguistic exchanges – as Lacan put it, dogs are neurotic, hystericized by language, without being its subjects. So they are not simply outside language: what they can experience is a frustration that they cannot find their place within language, that they cannot inscribe their subjective position into it. This is where human curses and exclamation come in: they don't simply express our fear or anger or joy, but a much more basic frustration at the impossibility of saying in clear language what we want to say, of 'find[ing] the right word', as Aaron Schuster puts it:

> If a dog could speak, would he not bellow a curse? [. . .] To speak is to tarry with the impossibility of speaking, to give voice to and do something with the bewilderment, lassitude, and rage—the abject objecthood—in which Sartre's dog can only helplessly languish. To enter the symbolic order doesn't mean to simply

> leave behind the pet animal's protosymbolic confusion and take up one's place in behind the pet animal's culture. Rather it is to raise this impasse to the level of the word, and thereby subjectivize it. What Sartre describes as canine ennui ought to be understood as an essential moment in the becoming of the speaking being.[25]

As a further illustration Schuster mentions the famous 'all-fuck' investigation scene in *The Wire* (season 1, episode 4), a scene that I analysed in detail in an old book of mine.[26] In an empty ground-floor apartment where a murder took place six months previously, McNulty and Bunk, their sole witness a silent housekeeper, try to reconstruct how it happened, using only the word 'fuck'. They say 'fuck' thirty-eight times in a row, in so many different ways – it comes to mean anything, from annoyed boredom to elated triumph, from pain or disappointment or shock at the horror of a gruesome murder to pleasant surprise, and it reaches its climax in the self-reflexive reduplication of 'Fuckin' fuck!'. One can easily imagine the same scene in which each 'fuck' is replaced by a more 'normal' way of conveying the same thing: 'Again, just another photo!', 'Ouch, it hurts!', 'Now I got it!', etc. This scene works on multiple levels, but at its most basic, it shows a curse in the full multitude of its uses: the same word can function in such a dizzying array of ways precisely because this multitude is sustained by the frustrating impossibility of clearly expressing one's subjective stance. So this scene does not enact a metaphorical or reflective game adding another level to the 'realistic' functioning of language – on the contrary, it enacts the basic gesture of language, by bringing out the impossibility on which language is based: we use words in a language because the 'true' word is missing, and this word is missing because I – the speaking subject – don't have a proper place within the symbolic, because I am a crack in its edifice.

We can – should, even – imagine an ideal analytic session in which the analyst reenacts the scene from *The Wire* and from time to time just interrupts the patient's flow of words with a curse, maybe even with a simple 'Fuck!'. It is also in this sense that the analyst is the obverse of the master. The so-called 'pansexualism' wrongly attributed to Freud ('behind everything there is sex') would acquire in this way an unexpected meaning: yes, the analyst's reply to everything is 'Fuck!', but this fuck has nothing to do with sexuality, it can refer to anything and nothing.

And let's take this all the way, as far as we can: does the exclamation 'Christ!' not work in a similar way to 'Fuck!'? We can easily imagine the scene from *The Wire* with the 'Christ!' instead of 'Fuck!' where the curse would express the same frustrating inability to subjectivize our position in the big Other. And why should we not bring the two dimensions – sex and God's name – together? Recall (trigger warning!) the dirty joke in which a teacher asks an elementary school class how people go to heaven when they are dying, and one of the boys replies: 'First with our legs.' Surprised, the teacher asks why, and the boy replies: 'A week ago, when my father was on a business trip, I entered my parents' bedroom and I saw a man lying on my mother making strange movements; my mother's legs were raised high up and she was shouting: "Oh Christ, I'm coming!"' This mention of Christ is not simply a blasphemous punchline; it puts words to the mother's frustrating inability to find the right word for the intense pleasure she is experiencing. Even if Christ were not Christ, would he not also be justified in uttering a simple 'Christ' or 'Fuck!' instead of the well-known 'Father, why have you abandoned me' when dying on the cross? Only in Christianity can we imagine such an outcry.

To conclude, let us make it clear why swearing is an immanent part and sign of an authentic authority. In her *Disavowal*,[27] Alenka Zupančič rejects the commonplace that we live in an era in which all forms of authority are disintegrating; she focuses on the form of authority which is today stronger than ever, the authority of science. She begins by pointing out that its authority operates at two levels. Immanently, i.e., within the scientific discourse itself, a scientific endeavour gains its authority by way of surviving the test of refutability as defined by Karl Popper: if it survives this test, it is (for the time being) confirmed as true. Externally, science functions as an authority in social space: even those who do not understand a complex theory acknowledge it as true and relevant, i.e., as something that can be evoked as a justification of certain measures ('science has proved that we, humans, are also responsible for global warming'). At this level, however, critique of science intervenes with claims that scientific research was influenced or even controlled by the interests of capital which pushed scientists to ignore the ecological impact of human activity (or to exaggerate it), and to serve as an instrument of social domination.

Zupančič convincingly demonstrates that such a critique of science relies on a short circuit between the two levels: it pretends to undermine science from within while it brings out only its social status. It is not enough to say that scientists acted under the influence of the interests of capital; even if they did, their conclusions can still be true if we apply to them immanent criteria of scientific procedures. (But also the other way round: a science can advocate authentic emancipatory interests while it is scientifically worthless.) Furthermore, such a direct reference to the subjective corruption of scientists is too soft towards capitalism: it reduces to the psychological conditions of contingent individuals what is a feature of capitalism as a system, what belongs to its very notion (as Hegel would have put it).

To these two levels one should add a third one: what if scientific discourse (in the sense of modern science) is limited and constrained not just due to the external influence of social interests, but because this limitation is inscribed into its very form? As Lacan put it, the scientific discourse forecloses (excludes) the subject, it adopts a disinterested panoramic view on reality posing as 'objective science' while ignoring its own social mediation. The Frankfurt School Marxists endeavoured to prove that the basic procedure of 'objective science', its alleged social neutrality, practices what they called 'instrumental reason', reducing reality to an external object to be manipulated, and such an approach is possible only within a modern capitalist society. Marxism and psychoanalysis practice a totally different approach: they target a truth which can emerge only through radical subjective engagement, i.e., subjective engagement is not an obstacle to objective truth but its condition because the scientist itself is part of its object, not its external observer. In Marxism, a theory mobilizes its object, transforming it into a revolutionary subject, while in psychoanalysis, interpretation affects the object (the patient) if it is done at a right moment.

Such an engagement is only possible if we break out of today's liberal ideological universe in which permissiveness and free choice are elevated into a supreme value. In this universe, social control and domination can no longer appear as infringing on the subject's freedom: they are only permitted if they appear as (and are sustained by) individuals experiencing themselves as free. Unable to break out of this vicious cycle alone, as isolated individuals, since the more we act freely the more we get enslaved into the system, we need to be 'awakened' from this 'dogmatic slumber' of fake freedom from outside, by the push of a Master figure. This is why Isolde Charim is fully justified to characterize today's post-patriarchal narcissistic subject as a subject practicing voluntary servitude:[28] When I focus on my Ego, its potentials, interests and needs, I am far from being free, I remain enslaved to the socio-symbolic space within which my Ego was shaped.

A true Master doesn't try to guess what people want; he simply obeys his own desires so that it is for the people to decide if they will follow him. In other words, his power stems from his fidelity to his desire, from not compromising it. Therein resides the difference between a true Master and, say, a Fascist or Stalinist leader who pretends to know (better than the people themselves) what people really want (what is really good for them), and is then ready to enforce this on them even against their will. In short, in order for individuals to 'reach beyond themselves', to break out of their passivity and engage themselves as direct political agents, the reference to a Leader is necessary, a Leader who allows them to pull themselves out of the swamp like Baron Munchausen. Alain Badiou's thesis is that a subject needs a Master to elevate itself above the 'human animal' and to practice fidelity to a Truth-Event:

> The master is the one who helps the individual to become subject. That is to say, if one admits that the subject emerges in the tension between the individual and the universality, then it is obvious that the individual needs a mediation, and thereby an authority, in order to progress on this path. The crisis of the master is a logical consequence of the crisis of the subject, and psychoanalysis did not escape it. One has to renew the position

> of the master, it is not true that one can do without it, even and especially in the perspective of emancipation.[29]

And Badiou is not afraid to oppose the necessary role of the Master to our 'democratic' sensitivity: 'This capital function of leaders is not compatible with the predominant "democratic" ambience, which is why I am engaged in a bitter struggle against this ambience (after all, one has to begin with ideology).'[30] And we should go to the end here: one of the signs of such an authentic Master is that he swears – there is no authority without curses. Swearing is here not a 'personal touch', not an obscenity signaling the presence of a private person, it is an immanent feature of the engaged Master. Only experts do not need to swear, and that's why their authority is much more dangerous.

From Bad to Worse

Over the past decade, Islamist insurgents linked to AQIM (al-Qaeda in the Islamic Maghreb) have staged a series of military coups in central Africa – Niger, Mali, Burkina Faso – with the open support of Russians from the Wagner group. The world media have told two stories about these events. Pro-Russian outlets interpret these events as a popular rebellion against French neocolonialism linked to local corrupted elites. The Western big media sees in them a large-scale plot by AQIM and Russia to establish an anti-Western and anti-liberal empire in central Africa. Both stories are true . . . up to a point.

France have continued to exert a subtle (or sometimes not-so-subtle) neocolonial rule over its African ex-colonies. After France granted independence to its Western and Central African colonies peacefully in the 1960s, it continued to exercise economic, political, and military influence in *la Françafrique*. France retains the largest military presence in Africa of any former colonial power; it forces African countries to give preference to French interests and companies in terms of public procurement and public bidding. It imposed on its former possessions the African Financial Community (CFA) monetary zone, which is inherently unequal and rooted in exploitative practices.[1]

However, it could also be argued that the uprisings in central Africa which have positioned themselves as 'anti-colonial' leave nations such as Niger, Mali and Burkina Faso even worse off than they were under French neocolonialism. Do these nations face futures in which they struggle with the same intractable problems facing the likes of Zimbabwe and Myanmar: authoritarian military rule, economic regression into new lows of poverty in which only the corrupt elite have access to wealth, political and social discourse gripped by an ideological fundamentalism which stigmatizes such things as equal rights for LGBTQ+ people as 'colonial' and thus deplorable? Emancipatory leaders like Thomas Sankara in Burkina Faso are a thing of the past, it seems. How can it be that much of Africa finds itself in such a desperate situation, where the only actual choice is between bad (Western neocolonialism) and worse (fake authoritarian anti-colonialism)?

One has to gather the courage here to reject the simple explanation that what is missing is the mobilization of the people, a true democracy sustained by popular engagement. If there is a lesson to be learned from the latest Right-populist protests, it is that the time has come to modify Abraham Lincoln's adage, 'You can fool all people some of the time and some people all the time. But you can never fool all people all the time.' In today's world, it might be more accurate to say, 'Most people can avoid being fooled some of the time and some people can avoid being fooled all the time. But most people are being fooled *all* the time.' A genuine emancipatory engagement with and for the people is a rare event and one which, historically, quickly disintegrates – and not only in the history of Western democracy, either. Recall how, in the time of the Cultural Revolution, Mao Zedong sent thousands of intellectuals to the agricultural communes to learn from ordinary farmers whom he elevated into 'subjects supposed to know' – one can argue that it was good for intellectuals to get acquainted with the lived realities of rural farm labour, but it would be a stretch to claim that deeper wisdom about social life would inevitably result. There is no one group, economically privileged or not, which possesses an authentic understanding of society.

There are two crucial steps we need to take in order to disrupt the notion of a hierarchy of understanding. The first is to dispel the myth of meritocracy: that whatever your social position at birth, society provides the opportunity and mobility necessary for talent and effort to rise to the top. In *Against Meritocracy*, Jo Littler demonstrated that meritocracy is the key cultural means of legitimation for contemporary neoliberal culture, and that whilst it promises opportunity, it in fact creates new forms of social division, since the structural inequalities of class, race and gender continue to play a much more important role than the apparent opportunities on offer.[2] One could also add to Littler's analysis a heterogeneous factor – that of chance. In *Success and Luck: Good Fortune and the Myth of Meritocracy*, Robert Frank, while not discounting the importance of hard work, shows that among groups of people performing at a high level, chance plays an enormous role in an individual's success.[3]

For most of the critics of meritocracy, the alternative is to trust that people, however manipulated and embedded in everyday ideology, however brainwashed by religious or ethnic fundamentalism, will eventually arrive at a spontaneous understanding of the justice and injustice on display in their social world. In short, many critics of meritocracy lean into a version of Lincoln's saying. Unfortunately, the complexity of today's global situation compels us to abandon the faith that people will come to a point of realization or recognition. For example, many people's hopes of averting total ecological collapse rest on the vague faith that 'people will act' before it is too late. But if the people who must act are comprised of individuals struggling with a cost of living crisis, bombarded by conflicting information on global warming – with even scientists and experts, who might be expected to hold authority, espousing radically divergent views about the nature of the problem, let alone what must be done to combat it – is it remotely realistic to expect that person to be able to act decisively in the world? When there appears to be no 'correct', definitive or clear answer to the ecological crisis, how can someone find the hope, faith or volition to subject themselves voluntarily to measures which in the short term promise to thrust them even deeper into poverty? I don't consider what people might call the 'intellectual elites' as immune to this same issue in any way. The endless loop of being unable to arrive at what Fredric Jameson called a proper cognitive mapping impacts us all. Nor is the solution to strive for a 'true' meritocracy; in order to achieve such a thing, our entire social order would have to be transformed.

To return to Abraham Lincoln's formulation, or its contemporary translation, it's not so much that the majority of people are fooled, it is basically that they don't care – their main concern is that their relatively stable life goes on undisturbed. The majority doesn't want actual democracy in which they would really decide: they want the *appearance* of democracy where they freely vote, but some higher authority which they trust presents them with a choice and then simultaneously shows then how they should vote. When the majority refuses to accept the hints and nudges from the status quo, confusion abounds; a situation in which they *do* have the power to decide is paradoxically experienced as a *crisis* of democracy, as a threat to the stability of the system. Furthermore, when people who have been made to feel like victims realize that they do have a choice, they often explode in real anger and things as a rule get much worse. The desire may be to have their voice heard, to have some say over their own lot, but as the ongoing wave of Rightist populism vastly demonstrates, this understandable desire exposes them even more fatally to manipulation, conspiracy theories and similar insidious narratives in which righteous frustrations are displaced on to blameless targets.

But is this all there is? An endless loop of ignorance, crisis, anger and conspiracy? Fortunately, I don't think so – there is a second step to be accomplished: one should accept that that, from time to time, in an unpredictable way, exceptions occur. The mist dispels, clarity prevails, the majority are mobilized for the right cause. Such moments are history at its purest – moments when years of change happen within the scope of a week (as it happened during the October Revolution). So, back to our starting point: Is there a chance that such a moment might occur in central Africa? If it did, the prerequisite would be that Western colonial forces rejected their own neocolonialism, which only serves to feed the false anti-colonialism of fundamentalist ideology. They would need to behave better than the bewildered individual we contemplated above, and sacrifice their own short-term profits in the interest of longer-term and perhaps less tangible gains. However, the Western colonial forces could only do this – turn against their own neocolonialism which feeds the false fundamentalist anti-colonialism – if they radically transform their own economy and gather the courage to rehabilitate the very concept of planning – a large-scale obligatory planning and not just vague 'coordination' or 'collaboration'. Such planning, which reaches well beyond the scope of single nation-states may appear unimaginable today, but there is simply no other way to confront the crises that pose a threat to our survival.

The first model of a Communist solidarity was enforced upon us by the Covid-19 pandemic: we were all aware that global mobilization and coordination were needed, as well as measures which clearly violated market rules (in the US, Trump passed a measure giving every family a sum of $2,000 and reactualized a law from the early 1950s, giving the federal government the power to determine what single industries would produce). This mobilization largely failed, but the only choice we have is to apply to it the old Beckettian motto: 'Try again, fail again, fail better.' If there is something of which we can be sure, it is that similar global emergencies will arise again, and we should prepare now for them.

We Are Biomass

If we take as our starting point that capitalism *isn't* the source of the asymmetries and imbalances in the world, it also means our goal shouldn't be to restore the 'natural' balance and symmetry. Such a project of restoring the pre-capitalist balance not only ignores (or underestimates, at least) the rift between humans and the natural world which is already at work in pre-capitalist societies: it also ignores the emancipatory dimension of the rise of modern subjectivity which leaves behind the traditional sexualized cosmology of mother earth (and father heaven), of our roots in the substantial 'maternal' order of nature. Marx's metaphor for capital is the vampire, the parasitic, predatory living dead sucking the blood of the living – in the topsy-turvy world of capital, the dead rule over the living and are, in some ways, more alive than the living. The implicit premise (or promise) of this metaphor is that revolution would reverse this hierarchy – to upend the state of things and by doing so, return to the normal, 'natural' order in which the living rule over the dead.

Lacan, however, teaches us that it is the inversion of the relationship between the living and the dead which defines what it is to be human in the first place: the 'barred' subject is the one who is undead, estranged from its biological substance, since it is enmeshed in the symbolic big Other which is a kind of parasite living off the humans who serve it. Enjoyment itself is something that parasitizes upon human pleasures, perverting them so that a subject can draw a surplus-enjoyment from displeasure itself.[1] In short, Lacan's well-known formula 'between the two deaths' (biological and symbolic) should be supplemented by its opposite: 'between the two lives'.

The primary characteristic of a radical ecology is, therefore, that it radically modifies the very notion of nature. In 'The Garden', a story by Afghan writer and poet Mozhgan Majoob published in the spring of 2024, the army builds a wall around a beautiful garden in order to isolate its beauty. But Darya, the heroine, has a dream which speaks to the failure of this barrier:

> If the animals and birds are united, together with the water, the plants and trees they can stop the army's walls from growing. The birds can fly above and past it, as I did in my dream, carrying seeds, while the snakes and animals burrow beneath it and make it weak, making room for the water to rush through and wash the walls away. The ants can eat whatever the armies try to build, and the bees buzz past carrying the pollen of every beautiful flower to grow inside and outside—to bury all of the walls that greedy people try to build. When nature is reunited, no human power is strong enough to defeat its unity.[2]

This last sentence has the cadence of wisdom, but I say it is as wrong as a human statement can be – what if (a part of) nature joins human destruction? Why is nature a harmonious, hegemonic whole? This is why we should reject the hidden anthropocentrism that pervades many deep ecological stances. Slovene biologist Eva Nadlučnik, who specializes in reducing suffering in animals, said recently in an interview for *Delo*: 'We should enable all animals to lead a dignified life.'[3] Compassionate as this aspiration sounds, its arrogance should also be noted: 'we' (humanity) are now given the task of diminishing the suffering of *all* animals *even when this suffering is not the result of how we (mis)treat them*. Moreover, what does a 'dignified life' mean to an animal? Is dignity not a specifically human quality or stance? Instead of getting lost in such speculations, we should rather focus on how contemporary history compels us to radically rethink our basic notion of life-world.

Let me begin by citing Michael Marder's 'Compassionate Genocide', well worth quoting because he moves beyond the expression of horror at what is taking place in Gaza to bring out the properly ontological implications of what we see when our screens bring us long drone shots of Gaza in ruins. It is a nightmarish vision 'where high-rise buildings and human bodies, ecosystems … and orchards are mutilated beyond recognition and reduced to organic-inorganic rubble'; the basic distinction between human bodies, the world they construct, and the 'natural' one they inhabit ceases to have any force. All are reduced to waste, horror, despair, the byproduct of destruction. In the face of this catastrophic mingling of the organic and the inorganic, the human, the natural and the artificial, Marder suggests that the only response is to abandon attempts to imaginatively identify with the victims of genocide in Palestine; a new kind of solidarity 'with dumpified lives, places and worlds' is needed:

> 'I am biomass' is a speech act that identifies with a vanishing life, with life's vanishing into dumped massiveness. The affirmation says: I am decimated being and stymied becoming, yet not exactly nothing. Dumped, I resist the dump with the surreal power of not-nothing. . . . [W]hat if Gaza were a condensed and particularly blunt version of a planetary tendency, as neoliberal newspeak with regard to 'compassionate genocide' leads us to believe? If so, then the biomassification of life, which proceeds at an uneven pace elsewhere, is accelerated in Gaza at the cutting edge of the most recent technologies of devastation. Rather than compassion, then, what is required is the solidarity of the dumped, who dare assert, 'We Are biomass.'[4]

When a wave of annihilation has passed over, whether that be in the form of genocidal conflict or ecological self-destruction, what is left – rubble, waste ground, a tangle of corpses and severed limbs – is *all* that is left on the basis of which to organize and connect. And the fact that something is left, abject and unwanted though it may be, can be a sort of basis for solidarity and resistance; the squashed dead birds of progress can unionize, the refuse can refuse to be ignored, even if the only compassionate witness is itself. At such a nadir, the neat divisions into organic/inorganic, alive/inert, human/not human no longer possess any relevance or force. Therein resides the key feature of the notion of biomass: in the ontological levelization in which domains that are totally different interact within the same space. The notion of biomass thus implies a crucial insight, as formulated by Levi Bryant:

> in an age where we are faced with the looming threat of monumental climate change, it is irresponsible to draw our distinctions in such a way as to exclude nonhuman actors.[5]

Bryant provides the convincing and pertinent example of ecological action in our capitalist societies: Why do all ideologico-critical calls fail to mobilize people? Why are the majority not engaging in serious action? If, in our approach to ideology, we remain at the level of so-called 'discourse analysis' and focus exclusively on the ideological motifs that are operative in our language games, this failure becomes inexplicable; but if we widen our focus and include other processes in social reality that influence our decisions – biased media reports, economic pressures on workers (threat of unemployment), material limitations, and so forth – the absence of engagement becomes much more understandable. Recall Jane Bennet's description in *Vibrant Matter* of how actants (anything which acts or to which activity is granted, with no implication of human agency or even human involvement) interact at a polluted rubbish dump; rotting trash, worms, insects, abandoned machines, chemical poisons, and so on each play their (never purely passive) role.[6] She concludes her book with what she calls (in no way only with irony) her 'Nicene Creed for would-be materialists':[7]

> I believe in one matter-energy, the maker of things seen and unseen. I believe that this pluriverse is traversed by heterogeneities that are continually doing things. I believe it is wrong to deny vitality to nonhuman bodies, forces, and forms, and that a careful course of anthropomorphization can help reveal that vitality, even though it resists full translation and exceeds my comprehensive grasp. I believe that encounters with lively matter can chasten my fantasies of human mastery, highlight the common materiality of all that is, expose a wider distribution of agency, and reshape the self and its interests.[8]

There is authentic theoretical and ethico-political insight to be gained by taking the role of actants seriously. If our ability to understand the environment as a biomass is triggered by a specific catastrophic event caused by humans, then, in Hegelese, only in such a context can 'biomass' become a concept-for-itself, part of our lived experience of reality.

We should bear in mind that Gaza in ruins is an extreme case of a biomass, one of the most profoundly horrifying and shocking images with which our media (social and otherwise) confronts us.

But there are also places throughout the globe where the distinction between the human and the non-human is pushed beyond breaking point: places where waste is dumped and thousands of people work separating glass, metals, plastic, etc. from chaotic heaps of rubbish – places where people nevertheless eat, breathe, live. Agbogbloshie in the suburbs of Accra (the capital of Ghana), called by the residents 'Sodom and Gomorrah', is one such example; the waste management system in Mumbai is another. The horrors experienced by those existing in a biomass environment are difficult to contemplate.

This does not render the biomass immune from exploitation. 'Reclaiming' these wastelands, breaking down what remains for material which can be reused without carrying the traces of its origin, is understandably attractive for ecological reasons, which only makes it more compatible with the preoccupations of technocratic societies. As Mark Wrathall argues in *How to Read Heidegger*, 'In the technological age, what matters to us most is getting the "greatest possible use" out of everything'.

Does this not throw a new light on how ecological concerns might enter an unholy alliance with the requirements of technology? Is the point of using resources sparingly, of recycling, etc., not precisely to maximize the use of everything? The huge masses of trash we find throughout the world could be viewed as the ultimate product of capitalism – useless computers, cars, TVs and VCRs. Spaces like the famous 'resting place' of hundreds of abandoned planes in the Mojave desert in California, where they are stored (supposedly temporarily) until they can be sold or scrapped,[10] confront us with the obverse truth of the capitalist dynamic, its inert objectal remainder. And it is against this background that one should read the ecological dream-notion of total recycling (in which every remainder is used again) as the ultimate capitalist dream, even if dressed up in the language of what is 'natural' and 'balanced'. In the dream of the self-propelling circulation of capital which would leave behind no material residue, we see the proof of how capitalism can appropriate even the most unlikely ideologies.

However, what makes the exploitation of a biomass different from business-as-usual capitalist logic is that it assumes a chaotic wasteland as our basic predicament, a wasteland which can be partially exploited but never abolished – as Marder put it, biomass is our new home, our being; we *are* biomass. This is why we can't simply avoid the horror of the biomass and exist in some 'natural', ecologically sustainable idyll. If only it was that easy! We need to affirm biomass as our only home and work within its confines, transforming it, engaging with it so we can experience a new harmony that pervades its very disturbing chaos. What if life as biomass forces us to reject the usual Leftist reordering of hierarchies and to open ourselves to what one cannot but call the *objective beauty* of reality (humans, animals, bacteria, decaying ruins . . .), leaving behind hierarchic order and existing in sameness and solidarity?

The End of the World

Images of the end of the world, imagined and otherwise, pervade our media. Alenka Zupančič noted ironically that one should not expect too much from the end of the world – it may disappoint us. I offer a similar sentiment, only phrased slightly differently: don't worry, sooner or later the end *will* come. This reassurance addresses the underlying belief that, if we talk and worry enough about the end of the world, it may *not* happen. This leads naturally enough to the question: What if the true end of time is not a mega-catastrophe but the endless repetition of the same endless deferred, and endlessly deferred, moment? A moment epitomized by the standard coda to an episode of a TV show, asking us to wait until next week (or in streaming life, simply the next episode) for the narrative to be continued – to quote Alessandro Sbordoni: 'As the end gets nearer, more is *yet to come*.'[1] So maybe we already live (in) the end of the world. An end which stretches on endlessly, with no possible resolution.

Russian-born French philosopher Alexandre Kojève, the great interpreter of Hegel in the 1930s, 1940s and 1950s, saw the 'end of history', the highest form of social order, take place first in Stalinist Russia and then in contemporary Japan. A Korean friend, Alex Taek-Gwang Lee, told me that, if Kojève were alive today, he would have chosen South Korea as an example of a place where history had ended, too. Why? It's impossible to answer this question without considering North Korea as well as South Korea, such is the nature of their hopeless entanglement.

Entanglement is at the heart of quantum physics and future quantum technologies. Like other aspects of quantum science, the phenomenon of entanglement reveals itself at very tiny, subatomic scales. When two particles, such as a pair of photons or electrons become entangled, they remain connected even when separated by vast distances: if one gives to one particle, say, an upwards spin, the other will enact a downward spin.[2] Are South and North Korea not entangled in a similar way, do they not function like a couple of entangled particles, embodying the poles of our global world, the two directions in which history could be said to have been trending, developed to their most extreme extent? Kojève should thus be supplemented here: it's not South Korea alone which stands for the end of history but the two Koreas together in their entanglement. The end of history is thus not a global peace but the point of an extreme and potentially self-destructive tension.

South Korea could be painted as *the* country of free choice – not politically, but in the sense of daily life, especially among the younger depoliticized generation. The choice we are talking about is the indifferent choice of moderate daily pleasures, the choice among options which don't really matter: what to wear that day, where to eat that evening, how to spend a lazy weekend. One could argue that the emerging generation mostly doesn't care about big issues like human rights and freedoms or the threat of war – while the world still pays attention to the aggressive pronouncements of the North Korean regime accompanied by nuclear threats, the large majority in South Korea simply ignore these threats. Since the standard of living of the large majority is relatively high, one can comfortably live in a bubble. The ritualistic consistency and slow, predictable rhythms of such a post-political, disengaged individual, ensconced in complacency that tomorrow will be much like today, were perfectly depicted by a recent Wim Wenders film, *Perfect Days* (incidentally a Japanese-German co-production). The protagonist, Hirayama (Kōji Yakusho), works as a toilet cleaner in Tokyo, fully content with the simplicity of his life. He follows a ritualized daily rhythm at work, listening to music in his free time, reading before bed every night. Japanese history and culture contains much about the benefits of slowness and peacefulness. Even the immensely popular Japanese eco-Marxist Kohei Saito (who is discussed in more detail elsewhere in this book) advocates slowing down (indeed his last book was called *Slow Down*).

The explosion in popularity of the so-called 'web soseol' (웹소설) over the past couple of decades speaks volumes about the depoliticized lifestyle and outlook of the younger generations in South Korea. These 'novels on the web' are all produced, distributed and consumed online, which has completely changed the existing publishing industry. The traditional protracted process of producing, distributing and consuming books now occurs almost simultaneously. Web novels are dominated by genre fiction – romances, detective novels, science-fiction and fantasy – and operate on a serialized model, with a new chapter released weekly. The popularity of this form of literature is gradually spreading outside South Korea, especially in China and the USA.

Web novels generate huge profits; bigger than Samsung, the largest South Korean corporation. As digital payment is easy and immediate, readers can enjoy web novels at a very low price (around 100 won – 0.07 Euros – per 'episode'), and since around ten companies are sharing the field, competition prevents centralized control. This is not the only way in which they are decentralized. Authors routinely engage directly with readers in the comments section. In this way, the 'web novel' has more in common with a traditional TV production model than the constant promise that the story is 'to be continued'; like network executives obsessively monitoring focus groups and ratings and tweaking the following week's episode to try to more precisely satisfy the capricious audience, authors can shape their texts in response to their audience. The directness of this interaction between author and reader problematizes traditional notions of authorship – who, in the end, is really writing this material?

'Web soseol' is often dismissed, if not actively deplored, as the end of 'proper culture', which probably has a great deal to do with the fact that by far the most popular genre of 'web soseol' (64 per cent of overall output) is romantic fiction and that 95 per cent of readers are women. Forms of popular culture which are generally consumed by women are usually the target of much handwringing and contempt, and romance as a genre generally dismissed as apolitical (as if marriage, the formation of family units, the negotiation of partnerships and relationships between the genders are not political!) and pure 'wish fulfilment' – a criticism which, in the case of 'web soseol', gains force from the direct interaction between producers and consumers under the auspices of big corporations. One could ask whether consuming 'web soseol' is so different, or so much less 'properly cultural' or 'political', from the types of cultural consumption common among younger generations in the West – or is it simply that we expect more political awareness, for political engagement to have more weight and urgency, in South Korea than in the UK or Western Europe?

A more interesting question is whether web novels produced and consumed in this way contain an unexpected emancipatory potential. Is destabilizing the relationship between author and reader not opening up spaces for new forms of creativity? Do many of the features of web novels not point to them as a new communist art form? A mostly anonymous crowd form spontaneous networks in which readers and writers engage directly and the production process is potentially collectivized – the figure of individual genius creator disappears, art loses its elitism and becomes a popular and collective process.

Ultimately one comes back to how 'web soseol' is being used, and to my eyes, it lacks the politicizing impact of some social media forms (see how Palestinians have used media to share videos of the atrocities in Gaza). What we see with 'web novels' in South Korea are depoliticized communities; while they are *ostensibly* more 'open' and agile, some very fundamental political aspects are missing from the form. And the form, certainly in its South Korean manifestation, is one which seems of a piece with the stability and weightless variety of choice which characterizes life as a younger person in South Korea.

North Korea is the precise opposite of this stability and weightless variety: permanent mobilization, a constant state of emergency, no free choice, life focused on how to confront the Enemy. One should note here that despite their seeming polarization, on a different level North Korea is nonetheless now moving in the same direction as the South: the regime has publicly announced that it is renouncing the goal of reunification with the South which was the very pillar of its politics for decades. South Korea was considered a part of the country occupied by a foreign country – the US – and the goal was to 'liberate' it. Now the North Korean elite is openly admitting that it is interested only in its own survival as the ruling clique. The basic opposition between the

North and the South, of course, remains intact: mobilization against the Enemy versus relaxed indifference. However, both extremes exist inside their own bubble: what they both exclude is a genuine politicization, an engagement and commitment to cope with global factors that threaten our survival.

Disavowal

Today, we are exposed to an entire series of traumatic and disturbing events: the catastrophic effects of climate change, wars, migrations, the disintegration of the social fabric that unites a society, the growing gap between the rich and the poor which threatens to trigger social upheaval ... Then there is the rise of the new far Right, manifested most recently in the string of victories for neo-fascist populist parties in western Europe: Italy, Netherlands, France ... So how should we (by 'we' I mean those who perceive these victories as a serious threat) react to this situation? The common-sense answer – keep a cool head, carefully analyse the situation and see what can realistically be done – is obviously too flat: everybody would in principle agree with it, which makes it toothless. A much better approach is to see what options are at our disposal. As far as I can see, there are three.

First: Outright denial. 'It's all overblown, let's just carry on with our lives as usual.' This strategy is mostly used by the new Right and its conspiracy theories (climate change denialism, vaccinations as the cause of autism, etc.), although recently Leftist versions have also begun to emerge (variations on the theme that the ecological panic, Covid pandemic, and the war in Ukraine are all inventions by big capital to keep workers under control).

Second: A fascination with the apocalyptic threat that accepts it as inevitable and something, perversely, which we are to enjoy. This stance is, of course, rarely formulated in an explicit way, but it often pervades our thinking as its obscure foundation.

Third, and most interesting: Disavowal. As Alenka Zupančič demonstrated, disavowal best renders the structure underlying our contemporary social response to traumatic and disturbing events, from climate change to unsettling tectonic shifts in our social tissue.[1]

Unlike denialism and negation, disavowal functions by fully acknowledging what we disavow – its logic is that of the well-known French phrase *je sais bien, mais quand meme . . .*, 'I know very well (that it's true), but all the same . . . (I don't really believe in it).' Such a stance is fast becoming the predominant mode in which we live our social and political lives. We see it lived out among the vast swathes of people who fully accept climate change and impending environmental collapse as scientific realities, but nevertheless continue to reproduce, drive cars, eat meat, rely on technologies and so on, just as if the planet's resources are limitless rather than exhausted: 'I know very well we are in serious trouble with our environment, but nonetheless . . . (life must go on, our individual desires are still worth pursuing, fundamentally it's business as usual).' Politically, we see it in the tepid response to the victories of neo-fascist parties and actors across western Europe: 'Yes, the rise of Rightist populism is a serious threat to our democracy, but nonetheless . . . (look at Italy, the Meloni government functions quite well in the EU context; even in Netherlands Geert Wilders' victory resulted in a respected technocratic government; and we can be sure that *Rassemblement National* in government will have to tone down its excesses, everyday things will continue as they always have, life must go on . . .).' Continuity, business as usual, an assumption that there's no meaningful alternative to continuing to behave as if tomorrow will not be materially different from today and that our way of life can endure indefinitely: these are the mechanisms of disavowal.

However, when the country went to the polls for the second round of the French elections on Sunday 7 July 2024, something totally different happened. Conventional wisdom was found wanting. Business was not conducted as usual.

The formula that best describes the success of the united bloc against neo-fascism is as follows: 'Of course we know very well that Marine le Pen's triumph is almost certain, the only open question is if she will get an absolute majority in the parliament, opinion polls are very clear, *but nevertheless . . .* (miracles happen, we may even win, we just have to work as fast and as hard as if there is still a realistic possibility of victory).' And this is what happened: not only did le Pen not get the absolute majority, her RN even finished third well behind the Leftist bloc and Macron.

Why did this apparently irrational strategy work? Because the knowledge contained in 'Of course we know very well' *is not neutral*: its objectivity is already biased. What we 'know very well', what is 'obvious', what is accepted as a matter of course, is not written in stone, but in shifting sand; it is a socially-constructed shared hegemonic opinion which obfuscates its owns cracks and inconsistencies in order to seem immutable, and our task is to change it. The point is not to provide 'alternative facts', but to undermine the framing that makes us select some facts and ignore others. This is why we are not dealing here with the usual disavowal but with a courageous act of taking a risk and ignoring our apparent limitations. Our stance should be: we know we appear weak and divided, but we should nevertheless do what has to be done. We know (or feel with the force of seeming knowledge) that we cannot avert environmental collapse, but we should still take the actions that would give us the best chance of doing so. In such a situation, where apocalypse is on the horizon, one should bear in mind that the standard logic of probability no longer applies – we need a different logic, that described by Jean-Pierre Dupuy:

> The catastrophic event is inscribed into the future as a destiny, for sure, but also as a contingent accident . . . [I]f an outstanding event takes place, a catastrophe, for example, it could not not have taken place; nonetheless, insofar as it did not take place, it is not inevitable. It is thus the event's actualization – the fact that it takes place – which retroactively creates its necessity.[2]

Dupuy provides the example of the French presidential elections in May 1995; here is the January forecast from the main polling institute: 'If, on next May 8, Ms Balladur will be elected, one can say that the presidential election was decided before it even took place.' Applied to the situation in France, this means: 'If there is economic chaos and social unrest, this will be necessary and inevitable; however, we could change the frame itself within which our fate seems predetermined.' This, according to Dupuy, is also how we should approach the prospect of an ecological or social catastrophe: not 'realistically' appraising the likelihood of the catastrophe, but accepting it as our fate, as unavoidable, and then, *on the basis of this acceptance*, mobilize ourselves to perform the act which will change destiny itself and thereby open up new possibilities within the situation. Instead of saying 'The future is still fluid, we still have time, time to act and prevent the worst', one should accept the catastrophe as inevitable – and then act to undo the destiny which is already 'written in the stars'.

The problem is, of course, what to do now that disavowal, in this particular case, worked? The predominant tone of the discourse responding to the defeat of le Pen is best rendered by a CNN headline: 'Macron's gamble has kept the far right out of power, but plunged France into chaos.'[3] The new conventional wisdom is that Emmanuel Macron and Jean-Luc Mélenchon (the key figure in the Left alliance) are so far apart politically that there seems to be no possibility of a compromise on which a viable coalition could be based. So, there will be prolonged instability which will for certain unsettle the economy and probably create the perfect conditions for a landslide *Rassemblement National* victory in the next elections. Ominous signs are already emerging but these signs are ambiguous – their meaning comes from the imagined/predestined catastrophe, and it is in our power to rewrite the past that leads to this future.

Notes

Progress and its Vicissitudes

1. Samuel Okiror, 'Uganda MPs revive hardline anti-LGBTQ bill, calling homosexuality a "cancer"', *The Guardian*, 1 March 2023 (https://www.theguardian.com/global-development/2023/mar/01/uganda-mps-hardline-anti-lgbtq-bill, last accessed 21 August 2024).
2. Karl Marx, 'The Future Results of British Rule in India', *New York Daily Tribune*, 8 August 1853, accessed via marxists.org (https://www.marxists.org/archive/marx/works/1853/07/22.htm, last accessed 21 August 2024).
3. Karl Marx, 'The British Rule in India', *New York Daily Tribune*, 25 June 1853, accessed via marxists.org (http://www.marxists.org/archive/marx/works/1853/06/25.htm, last accessed 21 August 2024).
4. Friedrich Nietzsche, *Thus Spake Zarathustra*, quoted from *The Portable Nietzsche* (New York: Viking, 1968), p.130.
5. Wendy Brown, *Regulating Aversion: Tolerance in the Age of Identity and Empire* (Princeton: Princeton University Press, 2006), p.89.
6. See Chris Lau and Hassan Tayir, 'They used to work for China's biggest companies. Now they're doing manual labour', CNN.com, 20 July 2024 (https://edition.cnn.com/2024/07/20/economy/china-economy-employment-blue-collar-work-intl-hnk/index.html, last accessed 21 August 2024).
7. Immanuel Kant, 'The Conflict of Faculties', *Political Writings* (Cambridge: Cambridge University Press, 1991), p.182.
8. See Walter Benjamin, 'Theses on the Philosophy of History', *Illuminations* (New York: Schocken Books, 1969).

Against Progress

1. See camh.ca, 'Straight Talk – Oxycodone' (https://www.camh.ca/en/health-info/guides-and-publications/straight-talk-oxycodone, last accessed 7 August 2024).
2. See Kohei Saito, *Marx in the Anthropocene* (Cambridge: Cambridge University Press, 2023).
3. Karl Marx, 'Preface', *A Contribution to the Critique of Political Economy* (1859; Moscow: Progress Publishers, 1977), accessed via marxists.org (https://www.marxists.org/archive/marx/works/1859/critique-pol-economy/preface.htm, last accessed 7 August 2024).
4. Rafael Bernabe, 'Saito, Marx and the Anthropocene: A Critique', originally published in *Against the Current* (July-August 2023). Published on climateandcapitalism.com on 5 July 2023 (https://climateandcapitalism.com/2023/07/05/saito-marx-and-the-anthropocene-a-critique/, last accessed 7 August 2024).
5. Quoted in Carole Cadwalladr, '"Capitalism is dead. Now we have something much worse": Yanis Varoufakis on extremism, Starmer, and the tyranny of big tech', *The Guardian*, 24 September 2023 (https://www.theguardian.com/world/2023/sep/24/yanis-varoufakis-technofeudalism-capitalism-ukraine-interview, last accessed 7 August 2024).
6. See Todd MacGowan, *Capitalism and Desire* (Cambridge: Cambridge University Press, 2016).
7. Ven. P. A. Payutto, *Buddhist Economics: A Middle Way for the Market Place*, compiled by Bruce Evans and Jourdan Arenson, translated by Dhammavijaya and Bruce Evans (https://www.urbandharma.org/pdf/Buddhist_Economics.pdf, last accessed 7 August 2024).
8. Timothy Morton, *Ecology Without Nature* (Cambridge, MA: Harvard University Press 2007), p.35.
9. Ibid.

Acceleration

1. With reference to Gilles Deleuze and Félix Guattari's *Anti-Oedipus*. See Nick Land, *The Thirst for Annihilation* (London: Routledge, 1992).
2. See Land's collected writings: Nick Land, *Fanged Noumena: Collected Writings 1987–2007* (Falmouth: Urbanomic/Sequence Press, 2011).

3. See Nick Land, *The Dark Enlightenment* (*Studies in Reaction*, vol. 9) (Perth, Australia: Imperium Press, 2022).
4. Jean-Pierre Dupuy, *The War That Must Not Occur* (Redwood City: Stanford University Press, 2023, quoted from the manuscript).
5. Ibid.
6. Will Stewart, 'Nuclear war is the "inevitable" conclusion of the Ukrainian invasion, warns Russian general who wrote the nation's "war bible"', *Mail Online*, 5 September 2023 (https://www.dailymail.co.uk/news/article-12482085/Nuclear-war-inevitable-conclusion-Ukrainian-invasion-warns-Russian-general-wrote-nations-war-bible.html, last accessed 19 August 2024).
7. ET Online, '"Remove it across the world": Bhagavad Gita reference in "Oppenheimer" sex scene sparks outrage', *The Economic Times*, 23 July 2023 (https://economictimes.indiatimes.com/industry/media/entertainment/remove-it-across-the-world-bhagavad-gita-reference-in-oppenheimer-sex-scene-sparks-outrage/articleshow/102051810.cms?from=mdr, last accessed 19 August 2024).
8. Pjotr Sauer, 'Cuba uncovers "human trafficking ring" recruiting for Russia's war in Ukraine', msn.com, 5 September 2023 (https://www.msn.com/en-gb/news/world/cuba-uncovers-human-trafficking-ring-recruiting-for-russia-s-war-in-ukraine/ar-AA1gha7S?ocid=msedgntp&cvid=fe396f6e09d7445facbf288a32bbce3d&ei=9, last accessed 19 August 2024).

Holographic History

1. See Anil Ananthasawy, 'Is our universe a hologram? Physicists debate famous idea on its 25th anniversary', *Scientific American*, 1 March 2023 (https://www.scientificamerican.com/article/is-our-universe-a-hologram-physicists-debate-famous-idea-on-its-25th-anniversary1/, last accessed 10 August 2024).
2. Jonathan Watts, 'Climate engineering off US coast could increase heatwaves in Europe, study finds', *The Guardian*, 21 June 2024 (https://www.theguardian.com/environment/article/2024/jun/21/climate-engineering-off-us-coast-could-increase-heatwaves-in-europe-study-finds, last accessed 21 August 2024).
3. Lili Bayer, 'Europe must get ready for looming war, Donald Tusk warns', *The Guardian*, 29 March 2024 (https://www.theguardian.com/

world/2024/mar/29/europe-must-get-ready-for-looming-war-donald-tusk-warns, last accessed 21 August 2024).

4. Thomas Hertog, *On the Origin of Time* (London: Penguin, 2023), p.88.
5. Ibid., p.90.
6. Ibid., p.91.
7. I owe this thought to Jacqueline Rose.
8. Charlie Wood, 'How our reality may be a sum of all possible realities', *Quanta*, 6 February 2023 (https://www.quantamagazine.org/how-our-reality-may-be-a-sum-of-all-possible-realities-20230206/, last accessed 21 August 2024).
9. See David Graeber and David Wengrow, *The Dawn of Everything* (New York: Farrar, Straus and Giroux, 2021).
10. Walter Benjamin, 'On the Concept of History' (1940), translated by Dennis Redmond, accessed via marxists.org (https://www.marxists.org/reference/archive/benjamin/1940/history.htm, last accessed 21 August 2024).
11. Karl Marx, 'Foundations of the Critique of Political Economy', *Grundrisse* (1857-61; London: Penguin Books in association with New Left Review, 1973, translated by Martin Nicolaus), accessed via marxists.org (https://www.marxists.org/archive/marx/works/1857/grundrisse/ch01.htm#3, last accessed 21 August 2024).
12. See Pierre Bayard, *Le plagiat par anticipation* (Paris: Editions de Minuit, 2009).

Absolute Invariants

1. Tomasz Glen, 'The Albanian Prime Minister told a joke about Putin. The main character is Prigozhin', *Dnipro Today*, 7 September 2023 (https://www.dniprotoday.com/en/news/the-albanian-prime-minister-told-a-joke-about-putin-the-main-character-is-prigozhin-725, last accessed 12 August 2024).
2. David N. Mermin, *It's About Time* (Princeton: Princeton University Press, 2021), p.9.
3. 'Relativity of simultaneity', chemeurope.com (https://www.chemeurope.com/en/encyclopedia/Relativity_of_simultaneity.html, last accessed 12 August 2024).
4. Ibid.

5. Sabine Hossenfelder, *Existential Physics* (London: Atlantic Books, 2023), p.11.
6. Personal communication.
7. Mermin, *It's About Time*, p.177.
8. Ibid., p.181.
9. Hinze Hoogendorn, 'Perception in real-time: predicting the present, reconstructing the past', *Trends in Cognitive Science* 26.2, February 2022: 128-141 (https://psychologicalsciences.unimelb.edu.au/__data/assets/pdf_file/0006/4028505/Hogendoorn-TiCS-2022.pdf, last accessed 12 August 2024).
10. See 'Understand Albert Einstein's theory of relativity, about what is absolute and not relative', Britannica.com (https://www.britannica.com/video/185520/Description-theory-relativity-Albert-Einstein, last accessed 12 August 2024).

Worsting

1. See Jacques Lacan, . . . *or Worse: The Seminar of Jacques Lacan, Book XIX* (Cambridge: Polity Press, 2023).
2. See 'Marine Le Pen calls on "patriots" to build future majority government', *Guardian News* YouTube channel, 10 June 2024 (https://www.youtube.com/watch?v=SUAyCLsGlCo, last accessed 8 August 2024).

Concrete Analysis of a Concrete Situation

1. G.K. Chesterton, *Orthodoxy* (San Francisco: Ignatius Press, 1995), p.139.
2. V. I. Lenin, 'Notes from a Publicist: On Ascending a High Mountain' (February 1922), *The* Collected Works of Vladimir Lenin, vol. 33 (Moscow: Progress Publishers, 1965), accessed via marxists.org (https://www.marxists.org/archive/lenin/works/1922/feb/x01.htm, last accessed 19 August 2024).
3. Emma Graham-Harrison and Quique Kierszenbaum, 'Ex-Shin Bet head says Israel should negotiate with jailed intifada leader', *The Guardian*, 14 January 2024 (https://www.theguardian.com/

world/2024/jan/14/shin-bet-ami-ayalon-calls-on-israel-release-intifada-leader-marwan-barghouti, last accessed 19 August 2024).

4. Ibid.
5. Valerii Zaluzhnyi, 'Ukraine's army chief: The design of war has changed', CNN.com, 8 February 2024 (https://edition.cnn.com/2024/02/01/opinions/ukraine-army-chief-war-strategy-russia-valerii-zaluzhnyi/index.html, last accessed 19 August 2024).

Civil War

1. Antonio Gramsci, *Selections from the Prison Notebooks of Antonio Gramsci* (London: Lawrence & Wishart, 1971), p.276.
2. Anthony Zurcher, 'What Trump's guilty verdict means for the 2024 election', BBC.com, 30 May 2024 (https://www.bbc.co.uk/news/articles/cnll59r891xo, last accessed 21 August 2024).
3. Jennifer Agiesta and Ariel Edwards-Levy, 'CNN Poll: Percentage of Republicans who think Biden's 2020 win was illegitimate ticks back up near 70%', CNN.com, 3 August 2023 (https://edition.cnn.com/2023/08/03/politics/cnn-poll-republicans-think-2020-election-illegitimate/index.html, last accessed 21 August 2024).
4. This saying was first reported by Max Brod, in 'Der Dichter Franz Kafka', *Die Neue Rundschau* 32 (November 1921), p.1213.
5. Franz Kafka, *The Blue Octavo Notebooks*, edited by Max Brod (Cambridge, MA: Exact Change, 1991), p.41.
6. Quoted in Steven Müller-Doohm, *Adorno: A Biography* (Cambridge: Polity Press, 2005), p.438.

Authority

1. G.K. Chesterton, 'A Defense of Detective Stories', in H. Haycraft, ed., *The Art of the Mystery Story* (New York: The Universal Library, 1946), p.6.
2. 'What is robbing a bank compared with founding a bank?', Bertolt Brecht, *The Threepenny Opera* (1928), III.3, accessed via cuny.edu (https://blogs.baruch.cuny.edu/spring2017/files/2017/03/The-Threepenny-Opera-by-Bertolt-Brecht.pdf, last accessed 20 August 2024).

3. Søren Kierkegaard, *Fear and Trembling/Repetition: Kierkegaard's Writings*, vol. 6, edited and translated by Edna H. Hong and Howard V. Hong (Princeton: Princeton University Press, 1983), p.227.
4. Fredric Jameson, *Late Marxism. Adorno, or, The Persistence of the Dialectic* (London: Verso Books, 1990), p.30.
5. Jacques-Alain Miller, 'D'un autre Lacan', *Ornicar?* 28 (Paris: Navarin Editeur, 1984), p.55.
6. Jacques Lacan, *The Four Fundamental Concepts of Psycho-Analysis* (New York and London: W.W. Norton & Company 1978), p. 275.
7. See Jacques Lacan, *Le Seminaire, livre VII: L'Ethique de la psychanalyse* (Paris: Editions du Seuil, 1986), chapter XXI.
8. See Saul Kripke, *Naming and Necessity* (Cambridge, MA.: Cambridge University Press, 1980).
9. See Søren Kierkegaard, *Philosophical Fragments* (Princeton: Princeton University Press, 1992).
10. Søren Kierkegaard, 'Of the Difference between a Genius and an Apostle', *The Present Age* (New York: Harper Torchbooks, 1962), pp.100–1.
11. Ibid., p.105.
12. Ibid., p.98.
13. Ibid., p.102.
14. Jacques Lacan, *The Four Fundamental Concepts of Psycho-Analysis* (London: Tavistock Publications, 1979), p.220.
15. See John Austin, *How to Do Things with Words* (Oxford: Oxford Higher Education, 1973).
16. See John Searle, 'A Taxonomy of Illocutionary Acts', *Expression and Meaning* (Cambridge: Cambridge University Press, 1979).
17. John Searle, *Intentionality* (Cambridge: Cambridge University Press, 1983), p.172.
18. Jacques Lacan, *Le Seminaire de Jacques Lacan, livre XX: Encore* (Paris: Editions du Seuil, 1975), p.33.
19. Searle, *Expression and Meaning*, p.18.
20. See Lacan, *The Four Fundamental Concepts of Psycho-Analysis*, chapter 17.
21. See Austin, *How to Do Things with Words*.

22. See André Bazin and Eric Rohmer, *Charlie Chaplin* (Parcs: Éditions de Cerf, 1972).

23. The two most elaborate versions of this approach are to be found in Jürgen Habermas, *Knowledge and Human Interests* (Cambridge, MA: MIT Press, 1971), and in Helmut Dahmer, *Libido und Gesellschaft* (Frankfurt: Suhrkamp Verlag, 1972).

24. Søren Kierkegaard, *The Journals of Kierkegaard* (New York: Harper and Brothers, 1959), p.98.

25. Aaron Schuster, *How to Research Like a Dog* (Cambridge, MA: MIT Press, 2014), p.139.

26. See chapter 8 in Slavoj Žižek, *The Year of Dreaming Dangerously* (London: Verso Books, 2012).

27. See Alenka Zupančič, *Disavowal* (Cambridge: Polity Press, 2024).

28. See Isolde Charim, *Die Qualen des Narzissmus. Ueber freiwillige Unterwerfung* (Vienna: Zsolnay, 2022).

29. Eric Aeschimann, interview with Alain Badiou and Elisabeth Roudinesco, 'Appel aux psychanalystes. Entretien avec Eric Aeschimann', *Le Nouvel Observateur*, 19 April 2012.

30. Alain Badiou, personal communication (April 2013).

From Bad to Worse

1. See Isabelle King, 'True Sovereignty? The CFA Franc and French Influence in West and Central Africa', *Harvard International Review*, 18 March 2022 (https://hir.harvard.edu/true-sovereignty-the-cfa-franc-and-french-influence-in-west-and-central-africa/, last accessed 21 August 2024); and CaspianReport, 'France secretly owns 14 countries', CaspianReport YouTube channel, 24 February 2024 (https://www.youtube.com/watch?v=_-u1Pjce4Lg, last accessed 21 August 2024).

2. See Jo Littler, *Against Meritocracy* (London: Routledge, 2017).

3. See Robert H. Frank, *Success and Luck: Good Fortune and the Myth of Meritocracy* (Princeton: Princeton University Press, 2016).

We Are Biomass

1. I've dealt more in detail with this topic in the first chapter of my book *Surplus-Enjoyment* (London: Bloomsbury, 2023).

2. Mozhgan Majoob, 'The Garden', *Evergreen Review*, Spring/Summer 2024 (https://evergreenreview.com/read/the-garden/?emci=50366e26-e8df-ee11-85fb-002248223794&emdi=cfa86e30-81e0-ee11-85fb-002248223794&ceid=629579, last accessed 21 August 2024).
3. See (in Slovene) Saša Senica, 'Vsem živalim bi morali omogočiti dostojno življenje', *Delo*, 21 August 2024 (https://www.delo.si/novice/znanoteh/vsem-zivalim-bi-morali-omogociti-dostojno-zivljenje, last accessed 21 August 2024).
4. Michael Marder, 'Compassionate Genocide', *The Philosophical Salon*, 22 April 2024 (https://thephilosophicalsalon.com/compassionate-genocide/, last accessed 21 August 2024).
5. Levi R. Bryant, *The Democracy of Objects* (Ann Arbor, MI: Open Humanities, 2011), p.24.
6. Jane Bennet, *Vibrant Matter* (Durham, NC: Duke University Press, 2010), pp.4–6.
7. Op. cit., ibid.
8. Op. cit., ibid.
9. Mark Wrathall, *How to Read Heidegger* (London: Granta Books, 2006), p.102.
10. Zachary Franklin, 'Airplane Graveyards: Exploring the World's Abandoned Aircraft Cemeteries', EntireFlight.com, 22 October 2023 (https://www.entireflight.com/blogs/aviation-is-a-lifestyle/airplane-graveyards#:~:text=These%20facilities%20are%20usually%20located,Air%20Force%20Base%20in%20Arizona, last accessed 21 August 2024).

The End of the World

1. Alessandro Sbordoni, *Semiotics of the End: On Capitalism and the Apocalypse (Network Notion #1)*, published by the Institute of Network Cultures, 21 December 2023 (https://networkcultures.org/wp-content/uploads/2023/12/INC_nn1_Semiotics-of-the-End_Digi.pdf, last accessed 21 August 2024).
2. Caltech Science Exchange, 'What is entanglement and why is it important?', scienceexchange.caltech.edu (https://scienceexchange.caltech.edu/topics/quantum-science-explained/entanglement, last accessed 21 August 2024).

Disavowal

1. See Alenka Zupančič, *Disavowal* (Cambridge: Polity Books, 2024).
2. Jean-Pierre Dupuy, *Petite metaphysique des tsunami* (Paris: Seuil, 2005), p.19.
3. Sakya Vandoorne, 'Macron's gamble has kept the far right out of power, but plunged France into chaos', CNN.com, 8 July 2024 (https://edition.cnn.com/2024/07/07/europe/france-election-results-gamble-analysis-intl-hnk/index.html#:~:text—acron's%20gamble%20may%20have%20prevented,Olympics%20in%20three%20weeks'%20time, last accessed 7 August 2024).

Index